Introduction

The Texas Department of Public Safety, Driver License Division, is committed to creating a faster, easier, and friendlier driver license experience and a safer Texas. One step toward achieving these important goals is to continuously improve the *Texas Driver Handbook* by providing you with accurate information on traffic laws, clear images of road signs, examples of common driving situations, and general safety tips. We have also included special tips to emphasize important information you need to know.

Although the *Texas Driver Handbook* has been revised, its primary purpose remains the same: 1) to help you qualify for a Texas driver license, and 2) to help you become a safer driver.

The information contained in this handbook is not an official legal reference to Texas traffic laws. The information provided is only intended to explain applicable federal and state laws you need to understand in order to successfully operate a motor vehicle in Texas. If you would like to know the actual language of any traffic or criminal laws referenced in this handbook, please refer to the Texas Transportation Code and Texas Penal Code.

Once you receive your Texas driver license, keep this handbook as a reference on traffic safety and update it as needed. The Texas Legislature meets every two years and regularly makes changes to traffic laws. For the most current information on driver licensing, visit our website at http://www.dps.texas.gov/DriverLicense/.

Dear Texas Resident:

Operating a motor vehicle is an important privilege and responsibility for drivers, especially in a state as large as Texas with more than 314,000 miles of public roadways. Tragically, every year in Texas, approximately 3,500 people are killed in traffic crashes and more than 15,000 are seriously injured. Today, more than ever, drivers must avoid distractions in their own vehicle while also staying alert for impaired or unsafe drivers sharing the roadway – failing to do so could have tragic consequences.

The goal of the Texas Department of Public Safety is to provide you with critical safety information about driving in Texas in an effort to keep you, your passengers and other travelers safe on our roadways. Please carefully review and learn the information in this handbook, and always be mindful of the great responsibility that goes with obtaining a driver license and operating a motor vehicle in Texas.

Respectfully,

Freeman F. Martin
Colonel
Texas Department of Public Safety

Table of Contents

Chapter 1: Your License to Drive

Who May Drive a Motor Vehicle in Texas?

Individuals who meet the following criteria may drive a motor vehicle in Texas.

Residents:

- Texas residents who have a valid Texas driver license

- New residents who are exchanging a valid out-of-state license have 90 days to establish residency in Texas in order to secure a Texas driver license.

- Any person, while driving or operating any road machine, farm tractor, or implement of husbandry temporarily operated or moved on a highway is exempt from having a Texas license, unless the vehicle is a commercial motor vehicle

Nonresidents:

- Any nonresident who is at least 16 years of age and possesses a valid driver license issued in the nonresident's home state or Canadian province. Nonresidents at least 16 years of age who meet these criteria may drive a vehicle permitted to be operated with a Class C or Class M driver license in Texas

- Nonresidents who are at least 18 years of age may drive any vehicle in Texas if they are legally licensed to drive such a vehicle in their home state or country, and the home state or country grants like recognition (reciprocity) to citizens of Texas

Military:

- The driver of an official U.S. or state military service motor vehicle may drive a vehicle without a valid Texas driver license, unless the vehicle is a commercial motor vehicle

- A nonresident on active duty in the U.S. armed forces, the member's spouse, or dependent child who has a valid license issued by his/her home state

- Any person on active military duty who holds a valid driver license issued by the U.S. armed forces in a foreign country may drive a motor vehicle in Texas for 90 days from the date of their return to the U.S.

- Unless a license is suspended, cancelled, revoked or denied, a Texas driver license held by any person who enters or who is in the U.S. armed forces will remain valid as long as the:

    - Service continues; and

    - Person remains absent from Texas and the absence does not exceed 90 days from the date the licensee is honorably separated from service or returns to Texas

Special Note: You may not receive a Texas driver license until all valid driver licenses and IDs issued are surrendered.

Types of Texas Driver Licenses

Learner License (Instruction Permit)

A learner license, also known as an instruction permit, allows a student driver to legally practice driving when accompanied by a licensed driver. The licensed driver must be at least 21 years of age with at least one year of driving experience, must occupy the seat beside the driver, and cannot be intoxicated, asleep, or engaging in any activity that prevents observation and response to the actions of the driver. A learner license will indicate "Learner License" on the front of the card and expire on the minor's 18th birthday. A person applying for a learner license must:

1. Be at least 15 but no more than 18 years of age

2. Complete the classroom portion of a driver education course, vision exam, and knowledge exam

3. Meet all other requirements for a first time driver license (original) applicant

Table 1: Learner License

Minimum Age	Fee*	Expiration
15 with driver education	$15 for license + $1 fee = $16	For applicants less than 18 years of age, the license expires on their 18th birthday

*A $1 administrative fee is included in most transactions. However, if you are completing multiple transactions at the same time, either in-person, telephone or online, then you will only be charged the $1 administrative fee once. A $1 administrative fee is not charged for transactions made through the mail.

Applicants 18 years of age and older who wish to legally practice driving are issued a Class C license with the same restrictions as a learner license. The license is generally valid for eight years and costs $32 plus a $1 administrative fee.

Verification of Enrollment and Attendance (VOE) Form

If you are under 18 years of age and applying for your first Texas driver license, learner license, or provisional license, you must provide evidence that you:

1. Have obtained a high school diploma or its equivalent; or

2. Are a student enrolled in a public, private, or home school and attended school for at least 80 days in the fall or spring semester preceding the date of application; or

3. Have been enrolled for at least 45 days and are enrolled at the time of application in a program to prepare individuals to pass the high school equivalency exam.

This information is included on the Verification of Enrollment and Attendance (VOE) form issued by your school. Ask your school officials to complete and sign the VOE form. The VOE may not be dated more than 30 days before the date of application for a license during the school year or more than 90 days during the summer. The VOE must be presented to the license and permit specialist (LPS) when applying for an original or first time license.

Hardship License

A hardship license (previously known as Minor Restricted Driver License or MRDL) may be issued to a minor who establishes the necessity to drive and may have restrictions based on the qualifying hardship.

An application for a hardship license (DL-77) must be executed by an authorized adult on behalf of the minor. Both the adult and the minor must sign the form and present it in person at the driver license office. Only a parent, guardian, or person having custody of a minor may apply on behalf of a minor. If the minor does not have a parent, guardian, or custodian, then an employer or county judge may apply on behalf of the minor.

A person applying for a hardship license must:

1. Be at least 15 years of age but not more than 18

2. Complete and pass a driver education course (a driver education course includes both the classroom and behind the wheel phase), vision, knowledge, and driving exams

3. Meet all other requirements for a first-time driver license (original) applicant.

For more information, please visit our website, https://www.dps.texas.gov/DriverLicense/teenDriver.htm.

DPS may require supporting documentation or conduct an investigation to confirm the information provided on the application.

DPS will issue a hardship license if it is determined that:

1. Failure to issue the hardship license will result in an unusual economic hardship for the family of the minor applicant

2. The hardship license is necessary due to an illness, disability, or death of a family member

3. The hardship license is necessary because the minor applicant is enrolled in a vocational education program that requires a license for participation

4. A court order requiring the issuance of the hardship license is presented

Graduated Driver License (GDL)

Teenagers and young adults have the highest crash rates of all drivers, and motor vehicle crashes are the leading cause of death for U.S. teens. Young drivers make up 6.5 percent of the driving population but are responsible for 13 percent of fatal crashes. The Graduated Driver License (GDL) program eases teens into the driving experience by phasing in driving privileges and minimizing exposure to high-risk situations.

The GDL program applies to driver license applicants under 18 years of age and has contributed to a decrease in fatal crashes. As a part of this program, all new driver license applicants are required to pass a driving exam conducted at a driver license office or authorized testing facility.

The GDL program consists of two phases. Phase One applies to learner licenses. Phase Two applies to provisional licenses. All drivers less than 18 years of age must meet the licensing requirements for a learner license or provisional license, but they are also subject to additional requirements, including driver education and the GDL program.

Phase One: This phase requires applicants under 18 years of age to hold a valid learner, hardship, or combination of learner and hardship license for a minimum of six months prior to the issuance of a provisional license.

If your license is suspended during Phase One, then the initial six-month period is extended by the number of days of the suspension because your license is invalid during the suspension period.

A Texas learner license will be issued to new Texas residents who are at least 15 years of age, present an out-of-state instruction permit, and submit a VOE form. A Texas learner license must be held for six months from the date of issuance before the individual is eligible for Phase Two.

Phase One requirements do not apply to Class M (motorcycle) licenses. Under the GDL program, there is no minimum time a person must hold a restricted motorcycle license before applying for a Class M license.

Phase Two: Phase Two restricts the driving privileges of individuals until their 18th birthday following the issuance of a provisional license.

During Phase, Two these individuals may not drive a motor vehicle:

1. With more than one passenger in the vehicle under the age of 21 who is not a family member

2. Between midnight and 5:00 a.m. unless the operation of the vehicle is necessary for the driver to work, to attend or participate in a school-related activity, or due to a medical emergency

All drivers who are under 18 years of age are restricted from using a wireless communication device, including a hands-free device, except in case of an emergency.

Provisional License

A provisional license is a driver license issued to persons 16 to 18 years of age that has the Phase Two GDL driving restrictions applied. The license will be marked "PROVISIONAL" and expire on the license holder's 18th birthday. A person applying for a provisional license must:

1. Be at least 16 but not more than 18 years of age

2. Complete and pass a driver education course (a driver education course includes both the classroom and behind the wheel phases), vision, and driving exams

3. Have held a valid learner, hardship, or combination of learner and hardship license for at least six months

4. Meet all other requirements for a renewal driver license applicant

Out-of-State License Holders

Applicants who are at least 15 but less than 18 years of age and present a valid out-of-state instruction permit will be issued a Phase One learner license. Applicants who are at least 16 but less than 18 years of age and present a valid out-of-state driver license will be issued a Phase Two provisional license with passenger and time restrictions after successful completion of the driving exam. Applicants must meet all other requirements for a first-time (original) applicant.

All licenses issued to persons less than 21 years of age will be marked "UNDER 21".

Classes of Driver Licenses

Class A, B, C, and M driver licenses are issued to individuals who are exempt from obtaining or not required to obtain a commercial driver license (CDL). Most non-commercial driver licenses issued to persons 18 years of age and older are valid for eight years and cost $32 (a $1 administrative fee will be added to in-person , telephone and online transactions). Some applicants receive licenses with shorter terms due to restrictions including, but not limited to, verification of lawful presence, sex offender registration requirements, or being 85 years of age or older.

Individuals who operate any of the following vehicles are exempt from obtaining a CDL but may need a Class A or Class B non-commercial driver license because the type of vehicle driven still meets the definition of a commercial motor vehicle. For more information on commercial motor vehicles and requirements for a CDL, please visit our website, http://www.dps.texas.gov/DriverLicense/CommercialLicense.htm or see the *Texas Commercial Motor Vehicle Drivers Handbook*. You may download the handbook online at http://www.dps.texas.gov/internetforms/Forms/DL-7C.pdf.

1. A fire-fighting or emergency vehicle necessary for the preservation of life or property or the execution of emergency governmental functions whether operated by an employee of a political subdivision or by a volunteer firefighter.

2. A military vehicle or a commercial motor vehicle when operated for military purposes by military personnel, members of the Reserves and National Guard on active duty, including personnel on full-time National Guard duty, personnel on part-time training, and National Guard military technicians.

3. A recreational vehicle driven for personal use.

4. A vehicle that is owned, leased, or controlled by an air carrier and is driven or operated exclusively by an employee of the air carrier only on the premises of an airport, on service roads to which the public does not have access.

5. A vehicle used exclusively to transport seed cotton modules or cotton burrs.

6. A former military vehicle as defined by Texas Transportation Code 504.402(i) that is operated intrastate and not driven by an individual for compensation or in furtherance of a commercial enterprise.

7. A covered farm vehicle as defined by 49 CFR Section 390.5 that is used to transport agricultural commodities, livestock, machinery or supplies to or from a farm or ranch, not used in for-hire motor carrier operations and if under 26,001 pounds is operated anywhere in the United States and if over 26,001 pounds is operated within 150 miles of the farm or ranch.

8. A vehicle controlled and operated by a farmer:

   a. Used to transport agricultural products, farm machinery, or farm supplies to or from a farm

   b. Not used in the operation of a common or contract motor carrier, or

   c. Used within 150 miles of the person's farm.

Class A Driver License

A Class A driver license permits a person to drive:

1. Any vehicle or combination of vehicles described under a Class B or Class C driver license; and

2. A vehicle or combination of vehicles with a gross combination weight rating (GCWR) of 26,001 lbs. or more, provided the gross vehicle weight rating (GVWR) of the vehicle(s) towed is in excess of 10,000 lbs.

A Class A driver license does not permit a person to drive a motorcycle.

Table 2: Class A Driver License

Minimum Age	Fee*	Expiration
18 or older (Applicants 18 to 24 are required to successfully complete an approved driver education course.)	$32 for license + $1 fee = $33	Eight years
17 with completion of an approved driver education course	$15 for license + $1 fee = $16	On applicant's next birthday

*A $1 administrative fee is included in most transactions. However, if you are completing multiple transactions at the same time, in-person, telephone and online, then you will only be charged the $1 administrative fee once. A $1 administrative fee is not charged for transactions made through the mail.

Class B Driver License

A Class B driver license permits a person to drive:

1. Any vehicle included in Class C;

2. A single vehicle with a gross vehicle weight rating (GVWR) of 26,001 lbs. or more and any such vehicle towing either a vehicle with a GVWR that does not exceed 10,000 lbs. or a farm trailer with a GVWR that does not exceed 20,000 lbs.; and

A Class B driver license does not permit a person to drive a motorcycle.

Table 3: Class B Driver License

Minimum Age	Fee*	Expiration
18 or older (Applicants 18 to 24 are required to successfully complete an approved driver education course.)	$32 for license + $1 fee = $33	Eight years
17 with completion of an approved driver education course	$15 for license + $1 fee = $16	On applicant's next birthday

*A $1 administrative fee is included in most transactions. However, if you are completing multiple transactions at the same time, in-person, telephone and online, then you will only be charged the $1 administrative fee once. A $1 administrative fee is not charged for transactions made through the mail.

Class C Driver License

1. A single vehicle or combination of vehicles that are not included in Class A or Class B and

2. A single vehicle with a gross vehicle weight rating (GVWR) of less than 26,001 lbs. towing a trailer not to exceed 10,000 lbs. GVWR or a farm trailer with a GVWR that does not exceed 20,000 lbs.

3. An autocycle, defined as a motor vehicle, other than a tractor, that is:

   • Designed to not have more than three wheels on the ground when moving

   • Equipped with a steering wheel

   • Equipped with seats that do not require the operator to straddle or sit astride the seat

   • Manufactured and certified to comply with federal safety requirements for a motorcycle

A Class C driver license does not permit a person to drive a motorcycle.

Table 4: Class C Driver License

Minimum Age	Fee*	Expiration
18 or older (Applicants 18 to 24 are required to successfully complete an approved driver education course.)	$32 for license + $1 fee = $33	Eight years
16 with completion of an approved driver education course	$15 for license + $1 fee = $16	On applicant's 18th birthday
15 with the approval of a hardship license	$ 5 for license + $1 fee = $6	On applicant's next birthday

*A $1 administrative fee is included in most transactions. However, if you are completing multiple transactions at the same time either, in-person or online, then you will only be charged the $1 administrative fee once. A $1 administrative fee is not charged for transactions made through the mail.

Class M Driver License

A Class M driver license permits a person to drive a motorcycle. Before applying for a Class M license, you must pass a state approved motorcycle operator training course. Motorcycle training course providers require drivers who are less than 18 years of age to present proof of completion of the classroom phase of a driver education course, hold a learner license (issued after completing the classroom phase of a driver education course), or hold a valid Class C license prior to enrolling in a motorcycle operator training course.

Minimum Age

Motorcycle: 16 with completion of the classroom phase of a driver education course (32 hours) and a state approved motorcycle operator training course (16 hours).

Motorcycle of 250 cc or less: 15 years of age with DPS approval for a hardship driver license or completion of the classroom phase of a driver education course (32 hours) and a state approved motorcycle operator training course (16 hours).

For more information on Class M driver licenses, please visit our website, https://www.dps.texas.gov/DriverLicense/motorcycleLicense.htm

Table 5: Class M Driver License

Type	Amount	Expiration
18 and older	$32 for license + $1 administrative fee = $33	Eight years
Under 18	$15 for license + $1 administrative fee = $16	On applicant's 18th birthday
Add M	Add M to current license requires a $15 exam fee + $1 administrative fee = $16	Expires with license
Renewal	An additional $11 is required when renewing a Class M license + $1 administrative fee = $12	Expires with license

*A $1 administrative fee is included in most transactions. However, if you are completing multiple transactions at the same time, in-person, telephone and online, then you will only be charged the $1 administrative fee once. A $1 administrative fee is not charged for transactions made through the mail.

Fees and Driver Licenses for Veterans

Veterans who are honorably discharged and receive compensation for a service-related disability of at least 60 percent are exempt from paying driver license and ID card fees. Individuals applying for a CDL or who are required to register as a sex offender are not eligible for this fee exemption. The veteran must meet all other licensing requirements.

Designation on Driver License

DPS offers Veteran and Disabled Veteran designators with branch of service indicators on the face of the driver license and identification card (ID) for qualifying veterans. For more information on the veteran designations, visit our website at www.dps.texas.gov/DriverLicense/vetServices.htm.

Identification (ID) Cards

In addition to driver licenses, DPS issues ID cards with a photograph of the applicant. ID cards have a distinguishing number similar to a driver license and are maintained in the driver record file. ID cards are displayed in a vertical format for individuals who are younger than 21 years of age and are horizontal for individuals who are 21 years of age and older. Applicants must provide documents in accordance with DPS ID card policy requirements. For a list of acceptable documents to obtain an ID card, visit our website, http://www.dps.texas.gov/DriverLicense/applyforID.htm

Table 6: Identification (ID) Cards

Minimum Age	Fee*	Expiration
ID cards can be issued to any person of any age. Anyone under the age of 21 will have "Under 21" printed on the card.	$15 card + $1 fee = $16 (59 or younger)	Six years
	$5 card + $1 fee = $6 (60 or older)	

*A $1 administrative fee is included in most transactions. However, if you are completing multiple transactions at the same time in-person, telephone and online then you will only be charged the $1 administrative fee once. A $1 administrative fee is not charged for transactions made through the mail.

Medical and Emergency Information

On the reverse side of the card, state law requires DPS to print the statement **"Directive to physician has been filed at telephone #"** and **"Emergency contact number."** Space is provided on the surface for the license holder to write a telephone number.

Space is also provided on the card to allow individuals to voluntarily indicate if a health condition exists that may impede communication with a peace officer.

Additionally, an application for an original, renewal or replacement driver license or ID includes the option to provide the name, address and telephone number of two individuals who may be contacted in the event of injury or death of the applicant. Driver license and ID card holders may also add or update emergency contacting information online by visiting our website, https://www.dps.texas.gov/DriverLicense/emerContactInfo.htm.

Allergic Reaction to Drugs

DPS does not print medical information on driver licenses or ID cards. To add medical information to the back of your driver license or ID card, use a permanent ink pen and write the name of medication that may cause an allergic reaction.

Organ Donation

DPS offers "Donate Life Texas" pamphlets to any person who visits a driver license office. The pamphlets provide general information on the Donate Life Texas program. If you choose to be an organ donor, a small heart with the word "donor" will be printed on the front of the card. Cards that indicate a person's wish to be a donor shall be conclusive evidence of a decedent's status as a donor and serve as consent for organ, tissue, and eye donation. You can get more information and register to be an organ, tissue, and eye donor online at www.DonateLifeTexas.org.

Voluntary Contributions

If you are applying for an original or renewal driver license or ID card, you can voluntarily make a monetary contribution to the following programs:

1. The Blindness Education, Screening, and Treatment Program administered by the Texas Commission for the Blind, which provides screening and treatment for those individuals who are without adequate medical coverage.

2. The Glenda Dawson Donate Life Texas Program, which manages the donor registry and statewide donor education projects.

3. The Veteran's Assistance Fund, which provides grants to local government and nonprofit organizations to enhance or improve veteran assistance programs that address the needs of veterans and their families.

4. The Sexual Assault Evidence Testing Program, which helps fund the testing of sexual assault evidence (rape) collection kits.

5. The Identification Fee Exemption Account, which assists foster and homeless children and youths with payment of fees for driver licenses and IDs.

How to Obtain a Texas Driver License

If you are applying for a Texas driver license, you must comply with the following procedures.

Applying for a Texas Driver License

An application for a driver license must be made in person. You may obtain an application at any driver license office or download an application from our website at www.dps.texas.gov/DriverLicense/ApplyforLicense.htm.

All in-office applicants who are at least 17 years and 10 months old are provided the opportunity to complete a voter registration application.

All men 18-25 years of age who are U.S. citizens or immigrants are automatically registered for selective service upon issuance of an ID card or driver license.

Required Documents and Application Information

To apply for a Texas driver license, you must provide the following documents and information.

1. Your full name, proof of residential address, mailing address, current county of residence, place of birth, and date of birth

2. Identification documents

3. Social security number verified electronically through the Social Security Administration

4. Thumb or index fingerprints

5. Physical description

6. Answer the medical status and history questions listed on the application. Individuals with certain medical limitations may have their cases reviewed by the Medical Advisory Board (MAB) before the license is issued

7. Surrender any valid out-of-state driver license

8. U.S. citizenship status or lawful presence

For additional information and lists of acceptable documents, visit our website, www.dps.texas.gov/DriverLicense/ApplyforLicense.htm.

Driver Record

A complete record of all your examinations will be recorded on your application and scanned into the Driver License System where it becomes a part of your permanent driving record. Any convictions for moving traffic violations or crashes, including out of state records of convictions, will be recorded as part of your permanent driving record. To find out more information on driver records and how to obtain a copy of your record, visit http://www.dps.texas.gov/DriverLicense/driverrecords.htm.

Evidence of Financial Responsibility (Vehicle Insurance)

When applying for an original driver license, you must provide evidence of financial responsibility or a statement that you do not own a motor vehicle that requires the maintenance of financial responsibility.

Evidence of financial responsibility must meet at least the minimum amount required by Texas and cover each motor vehicle the applicant owns that requires maintenance of financial responsibility.

Vehicle Registration

When surrendering an out-of-state driver license, a new Texas resident must submit, with a driver license application, evidence that each motor vehicle owned by the person is currently registered in Texas, or indicate they do not own a motor vehicle required to be registered. A registration receipt issued by the county tax assessor-collector of the county in which the new resident resides is satisfactory evidence that your motor vehicle has been registered in Texas.

Fees

The required fee(s) must be submitted before any exams will be given for an original Texas driver license. An additional $1 administrative fee is included in most transactions. However, if you are completing multiple transactions at the same time, in-person, by telephone or online, you will only be charged the $1 administrative fee once. A $1 administrative fee is not charged for transactions made through the mail.

For more information on all fees, refer to Appendix D of this handbook or visit our website, https://www.dps.texas.gov/section/driver-license/driver-license-fees.

Driver Education

Individuals younger than 25 years of age are required to successfully complete an approved driver education course. For more information on licensing requirements for applicants younger than 25 years of age, visit our website at www.dps.texas.gov/DriverLicense/ApplyforLicense.htm.

Impact Texas Drivers (ITD)

All driver license applicants must complete the Impact Texas Drivers (ITD) course appropriate for their age group prior to taking the driving exam. For more information, visit the ITD website, https://impacttexasdrivers.dps.texas.gov.

Minors

If you are younger than 18 years of age, your application must be signed, under oath, by the parent or guardian with custody. If there is not a guardian, your employer or county judge may sign the application. The person who signs may ask DPS to cancel your license any time before your 18th birthday. This request must be in writing and sworn to before an officer authorized to administer oaths. In addition, the minor applicant and cosigner must acknowledge receipt of information that provides information about distracted driving and explains the zero tolerance law. *See Chapter 10: Alcohol and Drugs Impact on the Driving Ability* for more information.

Examinations

Before any exams are given, you must pay the required fee. Your picture will be taken and you will be given a payment receipt. If you do not pass the knowledge and driving exams on your first attempt, your application will be held for 90 days. After 90 days or three failed exams, a new application and fee will be required.

The knowledge and driving exams are not required for applicants 18 years of age and older who surrender a valid out-of-state license. After you have passed all applicable exams, you will be issued a temporary license, which you may use for 45 days or until you receive your permanent license in the mail. If you do not receive your license in 45 days, email our customer service center at https://www.dps.texas.gov/DriverLicense/customer_service/Other.aspx.

Part 1: The Knowledge exam

As part of the *Less Tears More Years Act*, all applicants younger than 25 years of age are required to take a driver education course to apply for a driver license. Upon successful completion of certain courses, the person is not required to take the Class C knowledge exam, also known as the written exam, at the driver license office.

There are three types of knowledge exams.

1. Class C – Knowledge exam for all original applicants

2. Class M – Motorcycle knowledge exam. This exam is waived for applicants who successfully complete a state approved motorcycle operator training course and present proof of completion.

3. Class A or Class B – Rules exam for operators of Class A and Class B vehicles

You must score a grade of 70 percent or better to pass any knowledge exam.

Part 2: The Vision Examination

Your vision will be examined when you are at the driver license office. Depending on the results, you may be required to wear corrective lenses while driving if the lenses improve your vision and help increase the safety of your driving. If the results are inconclusive, you may be referred to your doctor.

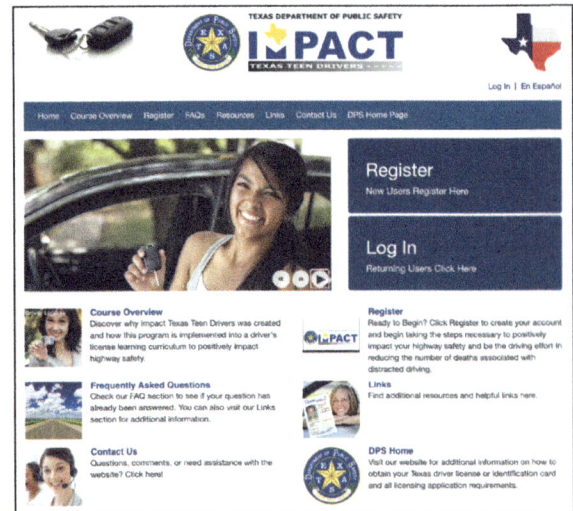

Part 3: The Driving Exam

The driving exam is given only after all other exams are passed and evidence of financial responsibility is presented or the vehicle is exempt under the Texas Motor Vehicle Safety Responsibility Act. The type of vehicle used for the driving exam must match the class of license on the application. No one younger than 18 years of age is exempt from taking the driving exam.

Individuals may take a driving exam at a driver license office or through a third party skills testing (TPST) school. The TPST program permits certain schools to administer the non-commercial driving exam.

Individuals who complete the state approved motorcycle operator training course are not required to take a driving exam for a Class M license if the person already has a valid, unrestricted Texas license. Individuals younger than 18 years of age must pass the motorcycle driving exam.

Additionally, the driving exam is not required for anyone applying for a learner license.

A $10 exam fee is required when changing from a lower to a higher class license or when removing restrictions from a license. The cost of adding a Class M to an existing license is $15.

Examples of Vehicles for Driving Exam

Class A Test in

Class B Test in

Class C Test in

Description of the Driving Exam

During the driving exam, you will not be asked to do anything illegal. You must follow all of the instructions given by the LPS. Do not carry on a conversation during the driving exam.

If you are not eligible to drive in Texas, a licensed driver must drive the car to the driver license office and exam area. If you are not issued a driver license then the licensed driver must also drive you away from the driver license office.

Upon completion of the driving exam, the LPS will explain all driving errors and let you know how to correct those errors.

Your application for a license will not be approved if you:

1. Violate the law

2. Refuse to follow instructions

3. Drive dangerously or have a crash

4. Have more than 30 points deducted on the driving exam

All drivers are graded on four basic skills, regardless of the type of driving exam.

1. Control – Your ability to make your car do what you want it to do

2. Observation – Your ability to see what other traffic is doing and other things that may create problems in traffic

3. Positioning – Your ability to drive in your lane

4. Signaling – Your ability to use turn signals as required

You may be graded on your performance on the following skills so it is good to practice before taking the driving exam.

a. Parallel parking (you may use the back-up camera on your vehicle for parallel parking; however, the use of an automated vehicle parking function will not be allowed)

b. Quick stop – You may be asked to stop your car as quickly as possible at about 20 mph without skidding your tires

c. Backing – Your ability to back the car for a distance of about 60 feet at a slow rate of speed and as straight and smooth as possible. Turn and look back at all times while backing or you may use the back-up camera and mirrors on your vehicle while backing; however, the use of an automated vehicle parking function will not be allowed

d. Stop signs

e. Traffic signals

f. Use of clutch – On standard transmissions, hold the clutch all the way down when starting the motor, shifting gears, when stopping, and once your speed drops below 10 mph. Do not drive with your foot resting on the clutch

g. Intersection observance – Use the proper lane; slow down and look both ways before entering the intersection

h. Turns

i. Right-of-way

j. Following, passing, and proper lane observance

k. Posture – Keep hands on steering wheel; don't rest your elbow on the window

Pass or Fail Driving Exam

If you do not pass the driving exam, you will need to schedule time for another driving exam. If you pass the driving exam, always carry your license with you when driving and upon request, show it to:

1. Any peace officer, sheriff, constable, judge, justice of the peace, or state trooper

2. Anyone with whom you are involved in a crash

Penalties for Driving Without a License

During a stop, a law enforcement officer will determine if you have a valid driver license as required.

Table 7: Penalties for Driving Without a License

Conviction	Penalty*
1st conviction	A fine of up to $200.
2nd conviction in one year	A fine of $25 to $200.
Driving without a license, operating a vehicle without insurance at the time of the offense, and driver causes a crash resulting in serious bodily injury or death	Class A misdemeanor punishable by a fine up to $4,000 and/or confinement in jail for not more than 365 days.

*Additional suspensions may apply.

Restrictions Placed on a License

A restriction may be placed on your license. This is not meant to interfere with your driving but to make you a safer driver. A complete list of restrictions can be found in Appendix 'XYZ' at the end of this handbook. This information is also available on our website at https://www.dps.texas.gov/DriverLicense/endrsRestrictions.htm.

Removing or Adding Restrictions

Visit your local driver license office for more information concerning the removal or addition of any restrictions from your driver license or learner license.

Replacement (Duplicate) or Change of Information on a Driver License or ID Card

You may be able to obtain a replacement (duplicate) card or change your address online at https://txapps.texas.gov/tolapp/txdl/. A change of address must be reported to DPS within 30 days. For more information and requirements, visit the website at https://www.dps.texas.gov/section/driver-license. The fee to replace or change information for online and in-person transactions is: $11 = $10 for license + $1 transaction fee.

If you are not able to use the online feature to change your address, you may mail an Application for Change of Address or Replacement (DL-64) to the address below. If you do not have the required DL-64, you can download the form from our website at https://www.dps.texas.gov/InternetForms/. Upon receipt of the $10 fee and completed form, a new license or ID card with the correct address information will be mailed to you.

> **Mailing Address:** Texas Department of Public Safety
> Issuance Services
> PO Box 149008
> Austin, TX 78714-9008

To change any other information on your driver license or ID card, you will need to visit a driver license office.

Out-of-State Licensees

If you are out-of-state but maintaining a Texas driver license, you may apply for a duplicate license by mail. Visit the website, https://www.dps.texas.gov/DriverLicense/nonmilitaryrenewal.htm to to download the appropriate forms and application. Complete and submit the required application with a $10 fee to:

> **Mailing Address:** Texas Department of Public Safety
> Issuance Services
> PO Box 149008
> Austin, TX 78714-9008

NOTE: Some driver licenses are not eligible for online, phone or mail-in transactions. These include limited term, sex offender and licenses issued to persons 79 years of age and older.

Renewing a License

A renewal notice invitation may be mailed to the last address you provided to DPS before your license expires. If you do not receive this courtesy notice, it remains your responsibility to renew your license.

Application for Renewal

A Texas driver license must be renewed every eight years. A renewal application must be made in person at any driver license office unless you are eligible to renew online at https://txapps.texas.gov/tolapp/txdl/, by mail, or by phone at 1-866-DL-RENEW. To check your eligibility to renew, visit us online or call the number provided.

A person must appear in a driver license office at least once every sixteen (16) years for a vision exam and to update the photo, signature and fingerprints. Please check the website at www.dps.texas.gov/DriverLicense/ to schedule an appointment at a location near you.

Alternate methods to renew will not be extended to:

1. Any person whose license is suspended, cancelled, revoked, or denied

2. Commercial driver license (CDL) holders

3. Holders of an occupational license, provisional license, or learner license

4. Licensees restricted because of driving ability or a medical condition that requires periodic reviews, including any medical or physical condition which may result in progressive changes to a licensee's ability to safely drive a motor vehicle

5. Driver license or ID card holders who are subject to sex offender registration requirements

6. Driver license holders who are 79 years of age or older

7. Driver license or ID card holders who do not have a social security number or photo on file

8. Non-U.S. citizens, due to a verification process

When you are at the driver license office you will be asked questions concerning your medical history. If you have certain medical limitations, your case may be referred to the Medical Advisory Board (MAB) for their opinion about how your condition may affect your driving. For more information on MAB, visit our website at http://www.dps.texas.gov/driverlicense/MedicalRevocation.htm

Individuals Returning to Texas from Military Service

Within 90 days of being honorably discharged, military personnel, spouses and dependents returning from active duty must present a Texas driver license and separation papers to obtain a renewal license without taking the knowledge and driving exams when the license has been expired for over two years.

Out-of-State Texas Licensees

Eligible individuals who do not currently reside in Texas but whose true, permanent home is in Texas may mail in their application for renewal. Visit the website, https://www.dps.texas.gov/DriverLicense/nonmilitaryrenewal.htm to download the appropriate forms and application. The following individuals who are out-of-state are not eligible to renew by mail and must renew in-person.

1. A person subject to sex offender registration requirements

2. A person 79 years of age or older

3. A person holding a commercial driver license (CDL)

4. A person who is not a U.S. citizen, unless active duty military

The proper fee and the results of your vision exam, performed by an eye specialist or an authorized driver license employee, must be included with your application. The license will be renewed and will be valid to expiration date shown or until 90 days after your return to Texas, whichever comes first.

Make check or money order payable to: TX DPS. Do not send cash. Mail to:

Mailing Address: PO Box 149008
Austin, TX 78714-9008

Suspensions and Revocations

Operating a motor vehicle is a privilege. If this privilege is abused, it may result in a driver license suspension or revocation.

Mandatory suspensions, revocations, and convictions for certain offenses involving fraudulent government records may require $100 reinstatement fee. There is also a $100 reinstatement fee for Drug Education Course. Administrative License Revocations (ALR) require a $125 reinstatement fee. Some mandatory suspensions also require filing a *Financial Responsibility Insurance Certificate* (SR-22).

Mandatory Suspension

Convictions for the following offenses will result in the automatic suspension of your license and driving privilege. For minors, see the *Suspensions and Revocations (Under 21)* section in this chapter.

1. Driving while intoxicated (DWI) by use of alcohol or drugs

2. Drug offense

3. Intoxication manslaughter or intoxication assault

4. Failure to stop and render aid

5. Causing the death or serious injury of anyone while operating a motor vehicle; involuntary manslaughter

6. Any offense punishable as a felony under the motor vehicle laws of Texas

7. Overtaking and passing a school bus (subsequent conviction)

8. Boating while intoxicated

9. Evading arrest

10. Driving while license invalid

11. Altered/unlawful use of a driver license

12. Displaying or possessing a fictitious or altered driver license or ID card

13. Lending a driver license or ID card to someone

14. Possessing more than one valid driver license or ID card

15. Providing false information or documents when applying for a driver license

16. Making, selling, or possessing a document deceptively similar to a driver license or ID card issued by DPS

17. Graffiti

18. Fictitious license plate, registration certificate, or safety inspection sticker

19. Fraudulent government records

20. Racing a motor vehicle on a public highway or street

Administrative Suspensions and Revocations

DPS has the authority to suspend or revoke a driver license or privilege of any driver, after an opportunity for a proper hearing, for any of the reasons listed below. A reinstatement fee is required for all discretionary suspensions and revocations.

1. Driving while license invalid

2. Causing a serious crash while driving a motor vehicle

3. Repeated violations of traffic laws, including:

    a. Four or more traffic convictions occurring separately within any 12-month period or

    b. Seven or more traffic convictions within any 24-month period

4. Failure to provide medical information or undergo examinations required by the medical advisory board (MAB).

5. Failure to take or pass a test when requested

6. Person has committed an offense in another state, which if committed in this state would be grounds for suspension or revocation

7. Violates a probation order set by a previous hearing

Suspensions and Revocations (Under 21)

Convictions or failure to comply with the following offenses will result in automatic suspension of the driving privilege of individuals who are less than 21 years of age (See Administrative License Revocation (ALR) section for more suspension information regarding minors.)

Alcoholic Beverage Code Offenses

1. Minor in possession

2. Attempt to purchase alcohol by a minor

3. Purchase of alcohol by a minor

4. Consumption of alcohol by a minor

5. Misrepresentation of age by a minor

6. Driving or operating a watercraft under the influence of alcohol by a minor

7. Failure to complete an alcohol awareness class

Health and Safety Code Violations

1. Failure to complete a tobacco awareness class when required

2. Drug offense

3. An offense under the Controlled Substance Act

4. A felony under Chapter 481 that is not a drug offense

Family Code Violations

1. Delinquent conduct by a minor or juvenile

Suspend or Revoke After Hearing of Minor

DPS has the authority to suspend or revoke the license or driving privilege of a minor after a proper hearing, for:

1. A juvenile court order

2. Failure to pay a fine or juvenile contempt, and

3. Two or more traffic convictions occurring separately within any 12-month period for a driver who is less than 18 years of age

Administrative License Revocation (ALR)

The Administrative License Revocation (ALR) law provides an administrative penalty for driving while intoxicated. A $125 reinstatement fee is required for all ALR suspensions.

DPS is authorized to suspend a license or driving privilege:

1. For individuals who are over 21 years of age who fail a breath or blood test (the blood alcohol content indicates a level of 0.08 or more)

2. Of any person who refuses to submit to a breath or blood test, or

3. For individuals who are under 21 years of age for any detectable amount of alcohol

Cancellations

DPS is authorized to cancel the driver license or ID card of individuals who do not meet certain qualifications. The following types of cases require cancellation of a driver license or ID card:

1. Suspension and revocation action from another state

2. Parental authorization withdrawn (for individuals who are under 18 years of age)

3. Failure to give the required information on the application for the license or ID card

4. Person is not entitled to the license or ID card

5. Incomplete driver education

6. False statement on an application for a license or ID card

Court-Ordered Suspensions, Revocations, and Cancellations

Upon receipt of a court order, DPS will suspend, revoke, or cancel a license or driving privilege for:

1. Delinquent child support

2. Requirement for an ignition interlock device (see https://www.dps.texas.gov/section/driver-license/ignition-interlock-devices for more information)

3. Failure to repay any overpayment of food stamps or financial assistance

4. Mentally incapacitated

5. Chemically dependent

6. Failure to renew their license annually as required (classified sex offender)

Denials

DPS is authorized to deny the issuance of a driver license to a person who is ineligible to receive a license in this state. An applicant may be denied a driver license for:

1. Suspension/revocation/cancellation/disqualification status in Texas, another state, or Canadian Province

2. Physical or mental incapacity preventing the safe operation of a motor vehicle

3. Acquiring motor vehicle fuel without payment

4. Certain criminal mischief (i.e. graffiti)

5. Purchasing or furnishing alcohol to a minor

6. Delinquent child support

7. Failure to pay reinstatement fees

8. Failure to appear or failure to pay for certain violations

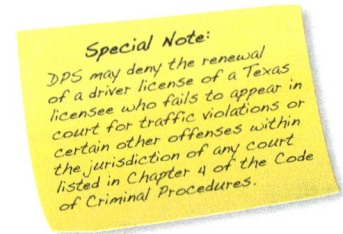

9. Drug offense

Special Note:
DPS may deny the renewal of a driver license of a Texas licensee who fails to appear in court for traffic violations or certain other offenses within the jurisdiction of any court listed in Chapter 4 of the Code of Criminal Procedures.

Driving While License Invalid (DWLI)

Individuals who drive a motor vehicle while their driver license is suspended, revoked, denied, or cancelled are subject to suspensions and criminal penalties. The penalties for driving a motor vehicle while your license is invalid are listed below.

Table 8: Penalties for Driving While License Invalid (DWLI)

Offense	Penalty
Driving a motor vehicle while driver license or privilege is suspended, cancelled, denied, or revoked.	Class C misdemeanor, punishable by a fine of up to $500.
The person has a previous conviction for the same offense, was operating a vehicle without insurance at the time of the offense, or the person's license had been suspended because of an offense involving operating a motor vehicle while intoxicated.	Class B misdemeanor, punishable by a fine of up to $2,000 and/or confinement in jail for not more than 180 days.
The person was operating a vehicle without insurance at the time of the offense and caused a crash which resulted in serious bodily injury or death of another. The suspension will automatically be extended.	Class A misdemeanor, punishable by a fine of up to $4,000 and/or confinement in jail for not more than 365 days.

Penalties for Non-Driving Alcohol-Related Offenses by Minors

The Zero Tolerance law provides penalties for minors who commit non-driving alcohol related offenses. A minor may not purchase, attempt to purchase, falsely state he/she is 21 years of age or older, or present a document indicating he/she is 21 years of age or older to a person engaged in selling or serving alcoholic beverages. A minor may not consume, or possess an alcoholic beverage. The penalties for non-driving alcohol-related offenses for minors are listed below.

Table 9: Penalties for Non-Driving Alcohol-Related Offenses - Minors

Offense	Penalty
1st offense	Class C misdemeanor punishable by a fine of up to $500, 8 to 12 hours of community service, and mandatory alcohol awareness course attendance. The driver license will be suspended (or privilege will be denied if not licensed) for 30 days.
2nd offense	Class C misdemeanor punishable by a fine up to $500, 20 to 40 hours of community service, and the minor may be required to attend an alcohol awareness course. The driver license will be suspended (or privilege will be denied if not licensed) for 60 days.
3rd offense (At least 17 years of age but less than 21)	Class B misdemeanor punishable by a fine of $250 to $2,000; minor may also be required to attend an alcohol awareness course. The driver license will be suspended (or privilege will be denied if not licensed) for 180 days. Minors are not eligible for deferred disposition on the third conviction or any subsequent conviction.
3rd offense (Under 17 years of age)	Class C misdemeanor punishable by a fine up to $500, 20 to 40 hours of community service, and the minor may be required to attend an alcohol awareness course. The driver license will be suspended (or privilege will be denied if not licensed) for 60 days, or the case can be transferred to Juvenile Court as delinquent conduct.

A minor who is convicted of driving while his/her license is suspended because of a non-driving alcohol related offense is subject to the penalties of Driving While License Invalid (DWLI).

Other Non-Driving Penalties for Alcohol-Related Offenses

A person, who purchases, furnishes, or sells an alcoholic beverage to a minor is subject to the penalties listed in the table below.

Table 10: Penalties for Purchasing, Furnishing, or Selling Alcohol to a Minor

Offense	Penalty
Purchased or furnished alcohol to a minor	A fine of up to $4,000 and/or confinement in jail for up to one year.
Sold alcohol to a minor	A fine of up to $4,000 and/or confinement in jail for up to one year.

Occupational License (Essential Need License)

An occupational license, also called an essential need license, is a special type of restricted license issued to individuals:

1. Whose driver license has been canceled, suspended, revoked, or denied for certain offenses (other than medical or delinquent child support); and

2. Who can prove to a court there is an essential need to drive.

Application for an occupational license is made to the district, county, or justice of the peace court in the precinct or county of the licensee's residence or to the court of original jurisdiction, whichever is applicable. If the court determines an individual is eligible for an occupational license, then a court order will be issued. The court order authorizes DPS to issue the occupational license. The applicant must submit the court order and all required items to DPS before an occupational license can be issued. The fee for this type of license is $10 for one year or $20 if authorized for two years. The court order may be used for 45 days for driving purposes while the occupational license is being processed. After 45 days, you must have both the court order and the occupational license in your possession.

A person issued an occupational license must also carry a certified copy of the court order when operating a vehicle and must allow a law enforcement officer to examine the order at the officer's lawful request. An occupational license may not be issued to drive a commercial motor vehicle.

For more information on occupational licenses, visit our website at
https://www.dps.texas.gov/section/driver-license/occupational-driver-license.

Chapter 2: Vehicle Inspection and Registration

Vehicle Inspection

All motor vehicles registered in Texas must be inspected each year at an official motor vehicle inspection station. This includes motorcycles, mopeds, scooters, and autocycles. Evidence of financial responsibility for the vehicle being inspected must be presented at the time of the inspection.

The Texas Department of Motor Vehicles (DMV) and the Texas Department of Public Safety (DPS) transitioned to a new vehicle inspection and registration system requiring motorists to display only the valid registration sticker on the windshield. The sticker serves as combined proof of registration and inspection.

When a vehicle passes inspection, the inspection station will print the passing Vehicle Inspection Report (VIR) and enter the information into an electronic database. The DMV verifies the database information at the time your vehicle is registered. You should still be prepared to present the printed VIR when registering your vehicle. The VIR is only valid for 90 days from the month of inspection for registration purposes.

Required Equipment for Vehicles

You must have the following equipment in proper working order for your car to be considered safe.

Table 11: Required Equipment for Motor Vehicles

Item	Description
Brakes	1. Foot Brake - Must stop car within a distance of 25 feet at a speed of 20 mph. 2. Parking Brake - Should be adequate to stop and hold car.
Lights	1. Two Headlights (one on each side of the front) - A beam indicator showing when the high headlight beam is on. 2. Taillights - All vehicles must be equipped with two taillights. Exception: Cars manufactured before 1960 are only required to have one taillight. 3. Brake (Stop) Lights - All vehicles must have two (2) working brake lights. Exception: Cars manufactured before 1960 are only required to have one (1) brake light. Vehicles equipped with a third or high mounted stop lamp require all three to be operational. 4. License Plate Light- A white light that lights the rear license plate when the headlights (or auxiliary lamps) are lighted. 5. Parking Lights - White or amber on the front, red to the rear (may be combined with other lights). 6. Reflectors - Two red reflectors, one on each side of the car (may be combined with taillights) must be placed at a height of 15 to 60 inches and be visible up to 600 feet; visible up to 350 feet on vehicles manufactured before 1960. 7. Turn Signals - Every motor vehicle, trailer, semi-trailer, and pole-trailer must have electric turn signals (except motorcycles and certain trailers). Exception: Passenger cars and trucks less than 80 inches in width and manufactured before 1960 are not required to have electrical turn signals.
Horns	Horns must be heard for a minimum distance of 200 feet.
Muffler and exhaust system	All 1968 or later models must be equipped with an exhaust emission system to help reduce air pollution.
Safety glass	New cars must be equipped with safety glass. Replacements of glass for any car must be with safety glass.
License plates	Vehicles must have one valid plate affixed to the front and one at the rear of passenger and commercial vehicles, in the manner prescribed by law, except dealer and commercial vehicles that are only issued one license plate.
Windshield wiper	Windshield wipers are necessary for safety in bad weather.
Rearview mirror	A rearview mirror must be able to reflect a view of the highway for a distance of at least 200 feet to the rear of the vehicle.
Slow moving vehicle emblem	Farm tractors and machinery, road construction machinery, animal-drawn vehicles and certain other motor vehicles assigned to travel at 25 mph or less must display the slow-moving vehicle emblem.
Front safety belts	Front safety belts are required if safety belt anchorages were part of the original equipment of the vehicle.
Tires	All vehicles are required to have tires in proper and safe condition with a minimum depth of 2/32 of an inch.
Fuel cap	The fuel cap on gasoline-powered vehicles from 2 to 24 years old will be checked to determine if the fuel cap is missing or defective. Exception: Antique vehicles, circus vehicles, slow moving vehicles, motorcycles, and vehicles operated exclusively by a fuel other than gasoline and vehicles newer than 2 years or older than 24 years.

For information on commercial vehicles, please see the special requirements section in the *Texas Commercial Motor Vehicle Driver Handbook*.

Equipment You Must Not Have

The following equipment is considered unsafe and is not allowed on your vehicle:

1. A red light showing from the front except on an emergency vehicle.

2. A bell, siren, or exhaust whistle except on an emergency vehicle.

3. A muffler cutout.

4. Anything extending more than three inches beyond the left side or six inches beyond the right side of the body, running board, or fenders of your car.

5. Flashing red lights on the front except on emergency vehicles, school buses, and church buses.

6. A radar interference device designed, manufactured, used, or intended to be used to interfere with, scramble, disrupt, or cause to malfunction a radar or laser device used to measure a vehicle's speed.

Minimum Road Clearance

A vehicle must not be modified or weighted in such a manner where the body is below the lowest part of the rims of the wheels.

Optional Equipment for Vehicles

The following equipment is considered optional and is not required to be on your vehicle.

Table 12: Optional Equipment for Motor Vehicles

Optional Item	Description
Spotlight	Spotlights must be turned off for a vehicle approaching from the opposite direction. If headlights fail, it may be used with the beam striking the road not more than 50 feet in front of the vehicle on which it is used.
Side cowl or fender light	Two of these types of lights are permitted; must show amber or white light without glare.
Running board courtesy lights	One running board courtesy light is permitted on each side; must show amber or white light without a glare.
Backup lights	Two backup lights are permitted separately or in combination with other lights. Do not use when vehicle is in forward motion.
Flashing lights	Widespread flashing lights may be used on any vehicle to warn of unusual traffic hazards; must show flashing amber or white to the front and flashing amber or red to the rear and must flash simultaneously.
Additional lights	Any motor vehicle may have up to three additional driving lights mounted on the front, not less than 12 inches but not more than 42 inches from the road surface.
Sunscreen or window tinting	If sunscreen or window tinting is used, it must comply with the appropriate state regulations for your vehicle make and model.

Registration of Vehicles

All vehicles must be registered in the owner's county of residency. Once the vehicle is properly registered, a registration sticker will be issued that must be displayed on the vehicle's windshield or on the rear license plate of a motorcycle or moped.

1. An owner must register a newly purchased vehicle within 30 days of purchase.

2. Nonresident truck owners may be issued 30-day temporary registration permits for certain movements of farm products and machinery during harvesting season.

3. Under certain conditions, temporary registration permits and reduced registration rates for special vehicles may be obtained.

4. Buyers' temporary tags are recognized for 60 days; dealers' metal registration plates may be used on any dealer-owned vehicle except for commercial purposes (vehicle inspection is required).

5. A manufacturer's metal registration plate may be used for vehicle testing purposes only; a vehicle inspection is required. Dealers temporary cardboard tags may be used for demonstrating a vehicle for sale, or for transporting or servicing vehicles without a motor vehicle inspection. These vehicles may not be used for driver license driving exams.

6. Farm registered vehicles, in addition to use for farm and ranch purposes, may be used as a means of passenger transportation for members of the family to attend church or school, to visit doctors for medical treatment or supplies, or for other necessities of the home or family. Farm registered vehicles may not be used for gainful employment.

7. For registration applications and detailed information, consult your County Tax Assessor-Collector or the Texas Department of Motor Vehicles (DMV).

Vehicles Not Required to be Registered or Inspected

The following vehicles are not required to be registered, inspected, or to display a license plate when temporarily operated on highways:

1. Farm tractors

2. Farm trailers, farm semi-trailers, and certain fertilizer and cottonseed trailers with a gross weight of 4,000 lbs. or less

3. Implements of agriculture

4. Power sweepers

5. Certain golf carts

6. Electric bicycles

7. Motorized and electric personal assistive mobility devices

When temporarily operated on highways, the following vehicles are not required to be registered or inspected if the owner annually secures a distinguishing $5 license plate and complies with other special conditions in the law:

1. Machinery for drilling water wells and construction machinery.

2. Farm trailers, farm semi-trailers, cotton trailers, cottonseed trailers, and certain fertilizer trailers weighing over 4,000 lbs. but less than 34,000 lbs gross.

Vehicle Registration for New and Nonresidents of Texas

A new Texas resident must register every vehicle he/she owns before applying for a Texas driver license.

When a nonresident establishes residency in Texas or enters into gainful employment, his/her vehicle may be operated for 30 days. After 30 days, the vehicle must be registered in Texas.

New residents registering a vehicle must obtain a Texas vehicle inspection report and verification of the vehicle identification number (VIN) by a state-approved vehicle inspection station prior to registration. The vehicle owner will then be provided the necessary form for processing the vehicle registration. Evidence of financial responsibility for the vehicle being registered must be presented at the time of registration. If evidence of financial responsibility is not presented, the vehicle cannot be registered. The registration receipt issued by the county tax assessor-collector for each vehicle will be acceptable proof of the registration when applying for a Texas driver license.

Chapter 3: Safety Responsibility

The Liability Insurance Law

The *Texas Motor Vehicle Safety Responsibility Act* was enacted to ensure all drivers are financially responsible for the death, injury, or property damage they may cause while operating a motor vehicle. All owners and/or operators of motor vehicles in Texas must have at least the minimum amount of liability insurance.

As of January 1, 2011, the minimum amount of liability insurance is:

- $30,000 against injury or death of one person
- $60,000 against injury or death of two or more individuals
- $25,000 against property damage

To comply with the *Texas Motor Vehicle Safety Responsibility Act*, a driver, unless exempt, must maintain liability insurance or be self-insured under the provisions of the Act. Evidence of financial responsibility must be presented at the time a person applies for a driver license, registers a motor vehicle, or obtains a motor vehicle inspection report.

Every owner or operator of a motor vehicle in Texas is required to furnish evidence of financial responsibility to a law enforcement officer upon request or to another person involved in a crash.

Evidence of Financial Responsibility

The following list includes items that will be accepted as evidence of financial responsibility.

1. A liability insurance policy in at least the minimum amounts.

2. A standard proof of liability insurance form prescribed by the Texas Department of Insurance and issued by a liability insurer that includes the:

    a. Name of the insurer, insurance policy number, and policy period;

    b. Name and address of each insured;

    c. Policy limits or a statement the coverage of the policy complies with at least the minimum amounts of liability insurance required by this Act; and

    d. The make and model of each covered vehicle.

3. An insurance binder indicating the owner and/or operator is in compliance.

4. A certificate issued by the state comptroller showing the owner of the vehicle has on deposit with the comptroller, money or securities for at least $55,000.

5. A surety bond issued by DPS showing the vehicle has a bond on file with DPS.

6. A certificate or copy of a certificate issued by the county judge of a county in which the vehicle is registered that shows the owner of the vehicle has on deposit with the county judge, cash or a cashier's check for at least $55,000.

7. A certificate or copy of a certificate of self-insurance, issued by DPS, which shows the person has more than 25 vehicles registered in his/her name.

8. An image displayed on a wireless communication device that includes the information required in a standard insurance form.

Failure to Provide Evidence of Financial Responsibility

If an individual fails to provide evidence of financial responsibility when required, he/she may receive a citation. The court may dismiss the charge if the individual provides evidence that a liability insurance policy was in effect when the citation was issued.

Upon conviction of driving a motor vehicle without sufficient evidence of financial responsibility as required, a driver is subject to penalties.

Table 13: Penalties for Driving Without Evidence of Financial Responsibility

Conviction	Penalty
1st conviction	A fine of $175 to $350.
2nd conviction and each subsequent conviction	Suspension of driver license, a fine of $350 to $1,000, and court-impoundment of the motor vehicle driven or operated by the person at the time of the offense provided the defendant was an owner of the vehicle at the time of the offense and is an owner of the vehicle on the date of conviction. The vehicle shall be impounded for 180 days. Before the court orders the release of the vehicle, evidence of financial responsibility must be presented to the court.

The vehicle registration, license or driving privilege of a driver will be suspended:

1. Upon conviction of a traffic violation that requires a suspension of a driver license, unless evidence of insurance is presented to DPS;

2. If a judgment resulting from a crash has not been satisfied within 60 days of the judgment;

3. If an installment agreement arising out of a settlement of a crash is in default;

4. If, while uninsured, the individual was involved in a crash in which another person was killed, injured, or there was at least $1,000 damage to a person's property and there exists a reasonable probability of a judgment being rendered against the driver; and

5. When required to maintain evidence of financial responsibility for two years from the most recent conviction date. More specific information about compliance with the Texas Motor Vehicle Safety Responsibility Act may be found online at https://www.dps.texas.gov/section/driver-license/financial-responsibility-insurance-certificate-sr-22. You may also write to:

Mailing Address: Texas Department of Public Safety
Enforcement and Compliance Service
PO Box 4087
Austin, TX 78773-0320

Chapter 4: Right-of-Way

At times, a driver must yield to others. There are certain rules to help determine who has the right-of-way; however, if the other driver doesn't follow these rules, give him/her the right-of-way. Remember, in every situation, right-of-way is something given, not taken. All drivers should know and understand the laws that determine who has the right-of-way.

Table 14: Penalties for Failure to Yield Right-of-Way

Offense	Penalty
Driver commits any traffic offense of which failure to yield the right-of-way to another vehicle is an element and causes bodily injury to another.	A fine of $500 to $2,000.
Driver causes serious bodily injury to another.	A fine of $1,000 to $4,000.

Right-of-Way at Intersections

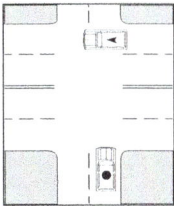

Intersections Controlled by Signs and Signals

When signs and signals control traffic at an intersection, you must obey them. Know the meaning of each sign and signal. See Chapter 5 for more information.

Single or Two-Lane Road Intersecting a Multi-Lane Road

If you are driving on a single or two lane road that intersects with a divided road or road with three (3) or more lanes, you must yield the right-of-way to vehicles traveling on the divided or three (3) or more lane road.

Unpaved Road Intersecting a Paved Road

If you are driving on an unpaved road that intersects with a paved road, you must yield the right-of-way to vehicles traveling on the paved road.

Intersections Not Controlled by Signs, Signals, Multi-Lanes, or Pavement

When approaching this type of intersection, yield the right-of-way to any vehicle that has entered or is approaching the intersection on your right. If the road to your right is clear or if approaching vehicles are far enough from the intersection to make your crossing safe, you may proceed. Since there are not any traffic-controls at this intersection, make sure there are no approaching vehicles from the left. You may legally have the right-of-way but be sure the other driver yields to you before you proceed.

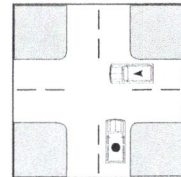

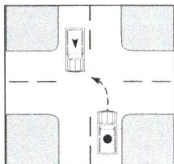

Turning Left

When turning left, always yield the right-of-way to any vehicle coming straight through from the other direction.

Private Roads and Driveways

When entering or crossing a road, street, or highway from a private road, alley, building, or driveway, you must stop prior to the sidewalk and yield the right-of-way to all approaching vehicles and pedestrians.

T-Intersection

When approaching an intersection of a through street traveling from a street that ends at the intersection, you must stop and yield the right-of-way to vehicles on the through street.

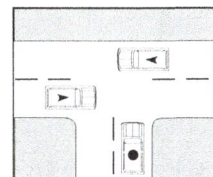

Enter or Leave Controlled-Access Highway

The driver traveling on a frontage road of a controlled-access highway must yield the right-of-way to a vehicle:

- Entering or about to enter the frontage road from the highway; and

- Leaving or about to leave the frontage road to enter the highway.

ONE-WAY FRONTAGE ROAD

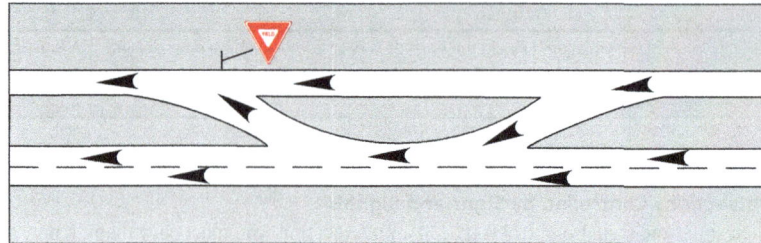

TWO-WAY FRONTAGE ROAD

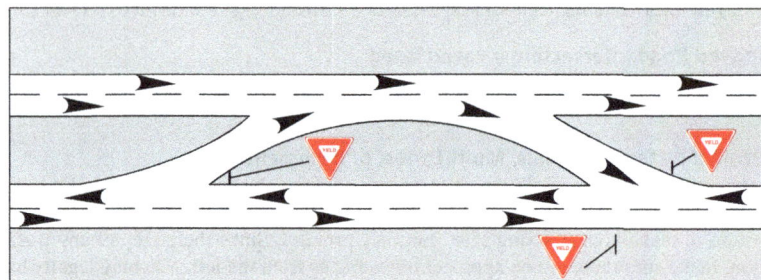

Driving on Multiple-Lane Roads

On a road divided into three or more lanes with traffic moving in the same direction, a vehicle entering a lane of traffic **from the right** must yield the right-of-way to a vehicle entering the same lane of traffic **from the left**.

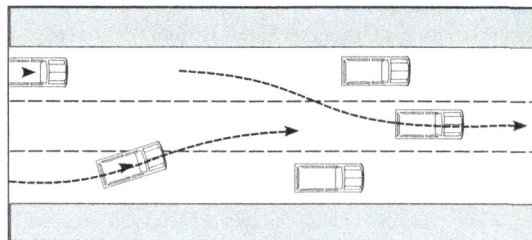

Railroad Grade Crossings

When approaching a railroad grade crossing, stop between 15 and 50 feet from the nearest rail if:

1. A clearly visible railroad signal warns of an approaching train

2. A crossing gate is lowered or a flag person warns of an approaching train

3. A driver is required to stop by an official traffic-control device or a traffic-control signal

4. An approaching train is within about 1,500 feet of the crossing. The train will produce an audible signal to identify the immediate hazard.

5. An approaching train is visible and in close proximity to the crossing

You are required to stop at a railroad grade crossing and remain stopped until allowed to proceed or it is safe to proceed.

A person who fails to obey the law regarding railroad grade crossings is subject to a fine of $50 to $200.

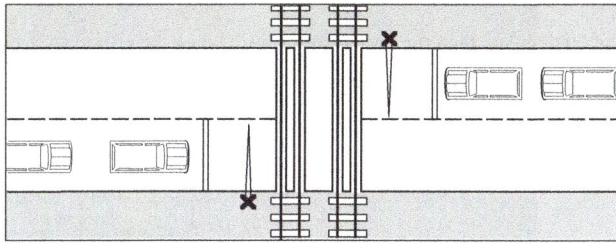

Additional Safe Driving Procedures at Railroad Crossings

1. If a railroad crossing is marked only with a cross-buck sign or reduce speed sign, then look both ways, and listen for a whistle. If a train is approaching, stop. If a train is not approaching, proceed with caution.

2. If red lights are flashing at a railroad crossing, stop. If a train is approaching, remain stopped until the train passes and the lights stop flashing.

3. If the railroad crossing gates have been lowered, stop. Remain stopped and wait until the train passes and the gates are raised before crossing.

4. Be sure the tracks are clear before you proceed to cross. There may be two or more sets of tracks. One train could be blocking the view of another.

5. Never stop on the tracks. If your car stalls on the tracks and you cannot restart it, get out and try to push the car off the tracks. If you cannot push the car off the tracks, get help. If a train is approaching and your vehicle is stalled, get out quickly and move away from the tracks. Run toward the approaching train to the side of the tracks and avoid flying debris.

6. Remember, trains do not and cannot stop at crossings. Trains always have the right-of-way.

7. Audible signs or whistles may be difficult to hear when approaching railroad crossings. Roll your windows down, turn your radio down, and listen carefully.

If you encounter a railroad grade crossing signal problem, call the Texas Department of Public Safety Communications Center at (800) 772-7677 or call your local police department or county sheriff's office. Each railroad crossing signal has an identifying number. Please note the number and be ready to provide it when reporting a problem.

Highway-Rail Grade Crossings Emergency Notification System (ENS)

The mission of the Federal Railroad Administration (FRA) is to enable the safe, reliable and efficient movement of people and goods for a strong America, now and in the future.

In Case of Emergency

- Locate the blue and white Emergency Notification System (ENS) sign at the grade crossing.

- Call for help! Call the railroad's emergency contact number listed on the blue sign.

- Communicate your location, by providing the identification number (see below) and state the nature of the emergency to the dispatcher.

1 Each railroad's emergency contact number,

2 The U.S. Department of Transportation (USDOT) National Crossing Inventory Number, which identifies the exact location of the crossing to the railroads.

The ENS sign includes: Emergencies and safety concerns at the grade crossing should be reported by using the information on the ENS sign.

For more information, visit www.fra.dot.gov

Yield Right-of-Way to Emergency Vehicles

You must yield the right-of-way to police cars, fire trucks, ambulances, and other emergency vehicles sounding a siren, bell, or flashing red light. If traffic allows, pull to the right edge of the road and stop. If you are unable to pull over to the right, slow down and leave a clear path for the emergency vehicle.

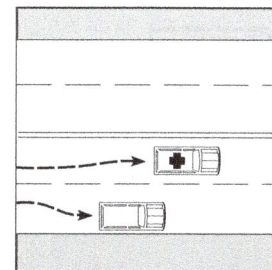

1. You are not allowed to follow within 500 feet of a fire truck answering an alarm or an ambulance when the flashing red lights are on.

2. Do not drive or park on the street where the fire truck has answered an alarm.

3. Do not park in a location that interferes with the arrival or departure of an ambulance to or from the scene of an emergency.

Unless otherwise directed by a law enforcement officer, drivers who approach a stopped emergency vehicle with its lights activated must:

1. Vacate the lane closest to the emergency vehicle if the highway has two or more lanes traveling in the direction of the emergency vehicle;

2. Slow to a speed not more than 20 mph less than the posted speed limit when the posted speed limit is 25 mph or more; or

3. Slow to a speed less than 5 mph when the posted speed limit is less than 25 mph.

Yield Right-of-Way to School Buses

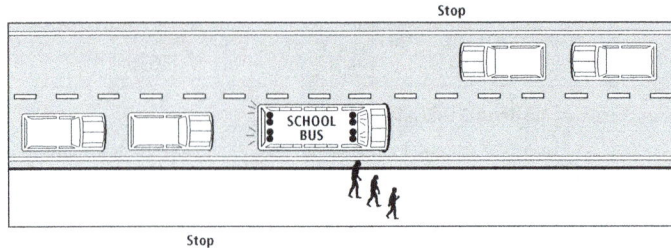

You must yield the right-of-way to school buses. Always drive with care when you are near a school bus. If you approach a school bus from either direction and the bus is displaying alternately flashing red lights, you must stop. Do not pass the school bus until:

1. The school bus has resumed motion;

2. You are signaled by the driver to proceed; or

3. The red lights are no longer flashing.

It is not necessary to stop when passing a school bus on a different road or when on a controlled-access highway where the bus is stopped in a loading zone and pedestrians aren't permitted to cross. A person who fails to obey the law regarding yielding the right-of-way to school buses displaying alternating, flashing lights is subject to the penalties listed in Table 17.

Table 15: Penalties for Failure to Yield Right-of-Way to School Bus

Conviction	Penalty
1st conviction	A fine of $500 - $1,250.
2nd conviction and every conviction after (within 5 years)	A fine not less than $1000 or more than $2000, possible suspension of driver license for up to six months.
Person causes serious bodily injury to another when passing a stopped school bus	Class A misdemeanor punishable by a fine of up to $4,000 and/or up to one year in jail.
Person causes serious bodily injury to another and has previously been convicted of passing a school bus and causing serious bodily injury	State jail felony punishable by 180 days to 2 years confinement and a possible fine of up to $10,000.

Yield the Right-of-Way to Pedestrians (Persons on Foot)

Avoid Turning a Car into a Deadly Weapon

You should always be on the lookout for individuals who are on foot (pedestrians) whether they have the right-of-way or not. Drivers must give the right-of-way to pedestrians:

1. At an uncontrolled intersection (there are not any traffic signs or signals for the pedestrian to enter the crosswalk)

2. If the pedestrian has a WALK signal or

   a. If there is not a pedestrian control signal, give the pedestrian the right-of-way on a green light.

   b. If the light changes after the pedestrian has entered the crosswalk, still give the pedestrian the right-of-way.

Yield Here to Pedestrian Signs

The "Yield Here to Pedestrians" sign is used when yield lines are used in advance of a marked crosswalk that crosses an uncontrolled multi-lane roadway.

In-Street and Overhead Pedestrian Crossing Signs

The "In-Street Pedestrian Crossing" signs or the "Overhead Pedestrian Crossing" signs may be used to remind road users of laws regarding right-of-way at a pedestrian crosswalk without signals.

The "In-Street Pedestrian Crossing" signs are placed in the road at the crosswalk location on the center line, on a lane line, or on a median island. The "In-Street Pedestrian Crossing" signs will not be posted on the left- or right-hand side of the road.

The "Overhead Pedestrian Crossing" signs are placed over the roadway at the crosswalk.

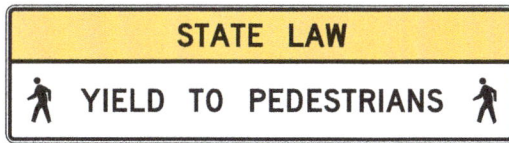

```
STATE LAW
👤 YIELD TO PEDESTRIANS 👤
```

Pedestrian Hybrid Beacons

A pedestrian hybrid beacon is a special type of pedestrian activated warning device used with signs and pavement markings to warn and control traffic at locations where pedestrians enter or cross a street or highway. Pedestrian hybrid beacons are only installed at a marked crosswalk.

Pedestrian Crossing Signals

What Drivers See	What Pedestrians See
Dark	Push the button.
Flashing Yellow	
Steady Yellow	
Steady Red	Start crossing.
Alternating Flashing Red Stop. Then go if clear.	*Flashing* Continue crossing.
Dark	

In-Roadway Lights

In-roadway lights are special types of lights installed in the roadway surface to warn roadway users they are approaching a condition on or near the road they may not see, which might require them to slow down or come to a complete stop. In-roadway lights are used as an alternative to traffic lights where pedestrian safety is a concern, and are typically placed at midblock crossings, school crosswalks, marked crosswalks on uncontrolled approaches, or in advance of roundabouts.

Image source: Some images in this chapter are courtesy of The MUTCD, 2009 Edition, published by FHWA at mutcd.fhwa.dot.gov/pdfs/2009/pdf_index.htm

Chapter 5: Signals, Signs, and Markers

Traffic Signals

Traffic signals help provide for the orderly movement of traffic. Drivers must obey these signals, except when a law enforcement officer is directing traffic. You must obey a law enforcement officer at all times when they are directing traffic even if he/she is telling you to do something which is ordinarily considered against the law.

Steady Red Light (Stop)

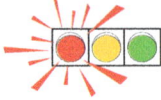

Stop before entering the crosswalk or intersection. You may turn right unless prohibited by law. You may also turn left if both streets are one way, unless prohibited by law. You must yield to all pedestrians and other traffic lawfully using the intersection.

A Flashing Red Light

Stop completely before entering the crosswalk or intersection, then proceed when you can do so safely. Vehicles on the intersecting road may not have to stop.

Steady Yellow Light (Caution)

A steady yellow light warns drivers to use caution and to alert them the light is about to change to red. You must STOP before entering the nearest crosswalk at the intersection if you can do so safely. If a stop cannot be made safely, then you may proceed cautiously through the intersection before the light changes to red.

A Flashing Yellow Light

A flashing yellow light warns drivers to slow down and proceed with caution.

A Flashing Yellow Arrow For Left-Turns

A flashing yellow arrow allows a driver to turn left, but the driver must yield the right-of-way to oncoming traffic.

Steady Green Light (Go)

A steady green light means the driver can proceed on a green light if it is safe to do so. You may drive straight ahead or turn unless prohibited by another sign or signal. Watch for cars and pedestrians in the intersection. Be aware of reckless drivers who may race across the intersection to beat a red light.

Green Arrow Displayed at the Same Time as a Red Light

A green arrow displayed at the same time as a red light means the driver can proceed carefully in the direction of the arrow after yielding the right-of-way to other vehicles and pedestrians.

Left Turn on Green

You can turn left on a green light. However, you must yield the right-of-way to all traffic that is approaching from the opposite direction before turning.

LEFT TURN
YIELD
ON GREEN

Traffic Signs

Traffic signs can help you to be a better driver because they:

1. Warn of hazards ahead that are difficult to see

2. Guide drivers to their destination by identifying the route

3. Inform of local regulations and practices

4. Regulate the speed and movement of traffic

The *Standard Colors* table shows colors commonly used on road signs and explains what each color means.

Table 16: Standard Colors

Color	Description
	Red: Stop, yield, or do what is posted on the sign
	Green: Indicated movements permitted, direction guidance
	Blue: Motorist services guidance
	Yellow: General warning or caution
	Black: Regulation
	White: Regulation
	Orange: Construction and maintenance warning
	Orange (Retroreflective): Used on various types of signs
	Brown: Public recreation and scenic guidance

Knowing the shapes of these signs will help you know what to do when you are approaching from a distance.

Table 17: Signs by Shape

Shape	Description
	Octagon: Exclusively for stop signs
	Horizontal Rectangle: Generally for guide signs
	Equilateral Triangle: Exclusively for yield signs
	Pennant: Advance warning of no pass zones
	Diamond: Exclusively to warn of existing or possible hazards on roads or adjacent areas.
	Vertical Rectangle: Generally for regulatory signs.
	Pentagon: School advance and school crossing signs.
	Round: Railroad advance warning signs.

Warning Signs

Warning signs alert drivers to conditions that are immediately ahead and tell them what to look for. There may be road hazards, changes in direction, or some other situation you should know about. Not only must warning signs be observed for safety reasons but to disregard them may be a traffic violation.

When you encounter a warning sign:

1. Pay attention

2. Follow instructions

3. Reduce speed to at least the posted speed signs

The following table provides examples of common warning signs.

Table 18: Warning Signs

Sign	Description	Sign	Description
	Warns of a traffic control signal ahead.		Road ahead makes a sharp turn in the direction of the arrow (right). Slow down, keep right, and do not pass.
 12'-6" LOW CLEARANCE	Height of underpass from road surface is shown. Do not try to enter if your load is higher than the figure shown on the sign.		There is a winding road ahead. Drive slowly and carefully, and do not pass.
	Advises you are approaching a section of highway where the opposing flows of traffic are separated by a median island.		The divided highway you are traveling ends ahead. Be careful as you approach the point where two-way traffic begins again.
	You are approaching a point where two roads come together and an additional lane begins. You are not required to merge. Watch for traffic in the new lane.		Slow down on wet road. Do not suddenly turn, speed up, or stop.
	The road curves one way (right) and then the other way (left). Slow down, keep right, and do not pass.		You should drive in the right-hand lane and expect oncoming traffic in the left hand lane.
	Another road enters the road you are traveling on from the direction shown. Watch for traffic from that direction.		Road ahead makes a gradual curve in the direction of the arrow (right). Slow down, keep right, and do not pass.
 ROUGH ROAD	Slow down, the road surface ahead is in poor condition.		Cross road ahead; slow down and watch for cross traffic. Look carefully in all directions for traffic.
	Cross traffic.		Gives advance notice of a reduction in the number of lanes of pavement ahead.

Table 18: Warning Signs (Continued)

Sign	Description	Sign	Description
	T-Intersection.		You are approaching a "T" intersection and must turn left or right. Be prepared to yield the right-of-way at the intersection if necessary.
	Y-Intersection or side road traffic to the right.		There is a low place in the road. Slow down in order to avoid losing control of your vehicle or an uncomfortable jolt.
	You are approaching a point where other traffic lanes come together with the one you are in. Watch for traffic from that direction.		Use extreme caution to avoid running off the paved portion of the highway, because the dirt on the side of the pavement is soft and may cause you to lose control of the car.
	You are near an area where a large number of pedestrians cross the street. Slow down and watch for pedestrians.		The bridge ahead is not as wide as the road. Slow down and use caution.
	You are near a school. Slow down, watch for children, and prepare to stop suddenly if necessary.		The road you are traveling on intersects a highway ahead. Slow down, look to the right and to the left for other traffic, and be prepared to stop.
	The surface of the road is covered with loose gravel. Go slow enough to keep complete control of your vehicle. Do not apply brakes suddenly or make sharp turns.		The road ahead makes a sharp turn to the right and then a sharp turn to the left. Slow down, keep right, and do not pass.
	Mounted in front of an obstruction which is close to the edge of the road, such as culverts, or center piers on divided highways.		Warns of hazardous condition on bridge caused by ice. This sign will be displayed continuously during winter time periods. Drivers should slow down, avoid applying brakes suddenly, or making sharp or sudden movements.
	Mounted immediately in front of an obstruction or at short changes in road alignment.		Used to indicate the alignment of the road as an aid to night driving.

Table 18: Warning Signs (Continued)

Sign	Description	Sign	Description
	Indicates traffic is permitted to pass on either side of a traffic island or an obstruction.		You are approaching a downgrade; all drivers approach with caution. It may be necessary to use a lower gear to slow your vehicle.
	Used to mark the ends of the side rails of narrow bridges and other obstructions.	RAMP METERED WHEN FLASHING	The sign will have yellow lights flashing (top and bottom) when the freeway ramp ahead is metered. The ramp meter (red or green) directs motorists when to enter the freeway.
	Slow your speed and watch for trucks entering or crossing the road or highway.	BUMP	There is a sudden high place in the road ahead. Slow down in order to avoid losing control of your vehicle or an uncomfortable jolt.
ROAD NARROWS	The pavement narrows ahead. Slow down and proceed with caution.		The road ahead curves sharply. Slow down, keep right, and do not pass.
	The hard-surfaced pavement changes to an earth road or low-type surface. Slow down.	LANE ENDS MERGE LEFT	The lane ends ahead. If you are driving in the right lane, you should merge into the left.
SHOULDER DROP-OFF	There is a significant drop from the pavement edge to the shoulder. If you must leave the pavement, slow down and steer firmly.		Be prepared for a stop sign ahead.
GROOVED PAVEMENT	The pavement has been grooved to lessen the possibility of slippery pavement in wet weather. Motorcyclists should use caution.		
	Slow down and watch for individuals who may be disabled or who may be crossing the road in a wheelchair.		

Regulatory and Warning Signs

Regulatory traffic signs instruct drivers what they should, or should not do, in certain circumstances. Drivers must obey all regulatory signs in the same manner as traffic laws. These signs help protect the safety of all road users. The following table provides examples of common regulatory and warning signs.

Table 19: Regulatory and Warning Signs

Sign	Description	Sign	Description
ONE WAY / ONE WAY	If you wish to turn at an intersection where this sign is posted, do so only in the direction indicated by the arrow.	STOP	Stop: A red stop sign with white letters or a yellow sign with black letters. The stop sign means come to a complete stop, yield to pedestrians or other vehicles, and then proceed carefully. Stop before the crosswalk, intersection, or stop sign. This applies to each vehicle that comes to the sign. Slowing down is not adequate.
HOV 2+ ONLY 6AM – 9AM MON–FRI	High Occupancy Vehicle (HOV) Preferential Lane: Buses and vehicles used for carpools may use this lane only between the hours of 6 a.m. to 9 a.m., Monday through Friday.	35 MPH (curve)	Advisory Speed Sign: This sign gives the highest speed which you can safely travel around the curve ahead.
DO NOT PASS / NO PASSING ZONE	Do Not Cross Yellow Lines: The distance you can see ahead is so limited that passing another vehicle is hazardous and you may not pass.	DO NOT PASS	Do not pass other vehicles.
ONLY (lanes)	This sign indicates two lanes of traffic are permitted to turn left. The traffic in the left lane must turn left, traffic in the other lane has a choice.	SLOWER TRAFFIC KEEP RIGHT	Stay in the right-hand lane if you are driving slower than other vehicles on the road.
RESERVED PARKING	Do not park, stop, or allow your vehicle to stand idling in a parking space reserved for disabled individuals unless your vehicle has a disabled license plate or windshield identification card.	EXIT 25 MPH	Indicates the speed at which the exit ramp from a highway may be traveled safely.
(No left turn)	Turning left at an intersection where this sign is posted is prohibited.	SPEED LIMIT 55	This sign tells you the maximum speed (in mph) you are permitted to travel. Sign also indicates the maximum speeds permitted on the road for day time and nighttime.
(No U-turn)	Making a U-turn at an intersection where this sign is posted is prohibited.	(No trucks)	Trucks are prohibited from using or entering the roadway where this sign is displayed.
WRONG WAY	If you see this sign facing you, you are driving the wrong way on a one-way street and you are directly opposing the flow of traffic.	(Keep right)	Drive to the right of this sign. This sign is used in advance of islands and medians.

Table 19: Regulatory and Warning Signs (Continued)

Sign	Description	Sign	Description
DO NOT ENTER	The road or street ahead is for one-way traffic traveling in the opposite direction. You must not drive in that direction or else you will be driving into oncoming traffic.	CROSSOVER	This sign marks a place where you may cross over to the other side of the divided highway.
YIELD	This signs tells you the road you are on joins with another road ahead. You should slow down or stop if necessary so you can yield the right-of-way to vehicles, pedestrians, or bicycles on the other road.	SCHOOL SPEED LIMIT 20 WHEN FLASHING CELL PHONE USE PROHIBITED UP TO $200 FINE	The use of a wireless communication device is prohibited in the school zone.
SCHOOL SPEED LIMIT 20 WHEN FLASHING	School Zone: The speed shown is in effect when the yellow light is flashing. Be extremely careful for school children.	4-WAY ALL-WAY	These signs are added to a stop sign advising that all approaching traffic to this intersection must stop before proceeding in the order you arrived. If two vehicles arrive at the same time, yield to the vehicle on your right.
PHOTO ENFORCED	Red light photo enforced.	LEFT LANE FOR PASSING ONLY	On roadways with more than one lane with vehicles traveling in the same direction, slower traffic should travel in a lane other than the farthest left lane. The farthest left lane is for passing only.
DO NOT CROSS DOUBLE WHITE LINE	Drivers should not change lanes or turn across the double white lines.	CENTER LANE ONLY	The center lane is only used for vehicles turning left, and should never be used for passing or moving through traffic. The only time a vehicle should enter the center lane is at a point where the vehicle will have time to slow down or stop to make a safe left turn.
PROTECTED LEFT ON GREEN ARROW	Vehicles facing the signal with the green arrow may proceed safely into the intersection. While turning left, you are protected from oncoming traffic that must stop for vehicles at an intersection. Vehicles turning at a protected light should use caution.	LEFT TURN SIGNAL	A green signal will indicate when you may turn left.
EMERGENCY STOPPING ONLY	This designates the shoulder of the road should only be used by vehicles required to stop because of mechanical breakdown, tire trouble, lack of fuel, or other emergencies.	RIGHT LANE MUST TURN RIGHT	Vehicles driving in the right lane must turn right at the next intersection unless the sign indicates a different turning point.
ROAD CLOSED	The road ahead is not open to any traffic. Look for a detour or other route.	25 MPH	Advisory Speed Sign: This sign gives the highest speed at which you can safely travel around the turn ahead.
FORM ONE LINE LEFT	Instructs drivers that all traffic on the same roadway must merge into one lane.		

Guide Signs

Guide signs are especially helpful when you are not familiar with an area. Guide signs tell you what road you are on and help you arrive at your destination safely. The table below provides examples of common guide signs.

Table 20: Guide Signs

Sign	Description	Sign	Description
LITTER BARREL 1 MILE	The only place where you may lawfully throw your trash on the highway is in a litter barrel. This sign advises that such a barrel is one mile ahead. Litter barrels are also found at all rest/picnic areas.	**EXIT ONLY**	The lane that has this sign above it exits ahead.
235 TEXAS	Texas Route Marker signs tell you what road you are or will be traveling on. Plan your trip and know which road you want to take.	**LOOP 270**	This sign tells you what road you are on. It is a short state highway in a city or urban area.
INTERSTATE 22	Interstate Route Marker signs tell you what road you are on. Plan your trip and know which roads you want to take.	**BUSINESS 22**	Indicates an officially designated highway that branches off the regularly numbered highway and goes through the business portion of the city.
79 SOUTH Daly	These signs are usually mounted above the road. The arrows indicate the lane or lanes to be used to follow a particular highway route.	**TROY 35 / UTICA 15 / ALBANY 30**	Travel information: This sign tells you which way to go and how far you must travel to get to cities, airports, and other destinations.
MILE 4 4	Mileposts provide a means of identifying the location of crashes, breakdowns, or other emergencies. Mileposts are erected every mile on interstate highways.	**X**	Lane-use control signals are overhead signals indicating if motorists should drive in a specific lane. If a red X appears above a lane, a driver should not drive in that lane. A steady yellow X means a driver should prepare to safely vacate the lane over which the signal is located because a lane control change is being made. A steady downward green arrow means a driver is permitted to drive in the lane over which the arrow signal is located. Lane-use control signals can be used on streets or highways.

Railroad Warning Signs

Railroad Crossing
This sign means you are within a few hundred feet of a railroad crossing. Slow down and be prepared to stop. If you see a train coming, STOP. Never try to beat a train.

Railroad Crossbuck
Railroad crossbuck signs are posted at every railroad, highway, road, or street grade crossing and show the location of the train tracks. If more than one track is to be crossed, the sign will show the number of tracks. Always slow down, look, listen, and be prepared to yield the right-of-way to an approaching train.

Emergency Notification System
Emergency Notification System signs are posted so the public may report unsafe situations and for railroads to respond to malfunctioning warning signals, vehicles stalled on the tracks or other emergency situations. Posted on each sign are an emergency contact number and U.S. Department of Transportation (USDOT) National Crossing Inventory Number. The inventory number identifies the exact location of the crossing.

Gate and Flashing Light

Stop when the lights begin to flash before the gate lowers across your side of the road. Remain stopped until the gates are raised and the lights stop flashing.

At railroad crossings stop within 15 feet to 50 feet of the nearest rail when:

1. You are directed to do so by a flag person

2. There are flashing red lights or warning bells sounding

3. There is any warning device telling you a train is coming

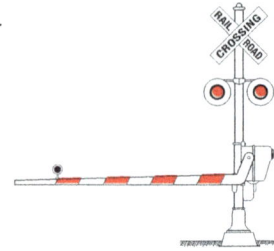

Pavement Markings

Pavement markings help you just like signs and signals. They are used to warn and direct drivers and to regulate traffic.

Two-Lane Rural Road with Two-Way Traffic

Keep to the right of the yellow center line. You may cross a broken line when passing another vehicle or when the right half of the road is closed. Do not cross the line if it is not safe or it is a solid yellow line.

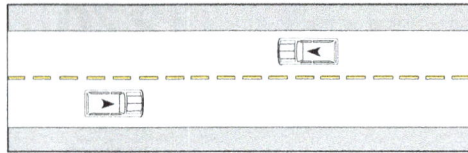

Three Lane One-Way Roads

When each lane on a one way road is marked with a broken white line, you may drive in any lane. When turning from a one-way road, make sure you move into the lane closest to the turn you are going to make well in advance of your turn.

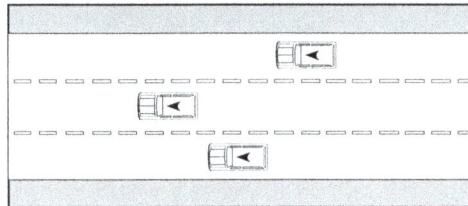

Left Turn Lane Only

The only time a vehicle should enter the center lane is at a point where the vehicle will have time to slow down or stop in order to make a safe left turn maneuver.

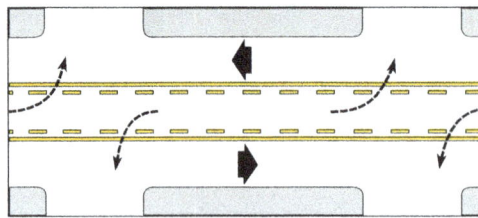

Left Turn Lane Only

Special Note: The center lane should never be used for passing or as a through-traffic lane.

Multi-lane Highway (Four or More Lanes)

Do not cross the double yellow line to pass. Stay in your lane as much as possible. If you are driving slower, keep in the right-hand lane.

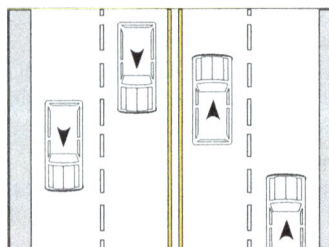

Solid and Broken Lines

A solid yellow line on your side of the road marks a "no-passing zone." Broken or dashed lines permit you to pass or change lanes, if safe.

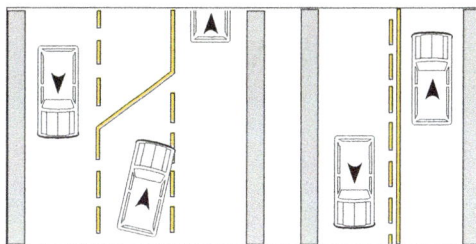

Crosswalks

White crosswalk lines are painted across a road to indicate pedestrian crossing areas. Pedestrians should use these areas when crossing the road. At intersections where stop lines are missing, you must stop before the crosswalk when required to stop by traffic signs, traffic signals, or pedestrians in the crosswalk.

White Stop Lines

White stop lines are painted across the pavement lanes at traffic signs or signals. Where these lines are present, you are required to stop behind the stop line.

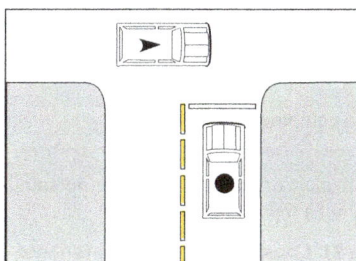

Solid Lines

Solid white lines are used for pavement edge lines, shoulder markings, channelizing, transitions, and lane use control. Crossing a solid white line should be avoided if possible. The solid yellow line on the left edge of the road is a guide for drivers to indicate driving to the left of the yellow line is prohibited. This type of yellow line can be found on interstate highways.

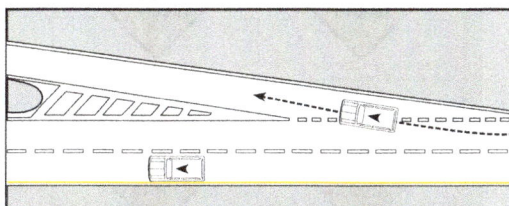

Crossing is prohibited where there is a pavement marking of double solid white lines.

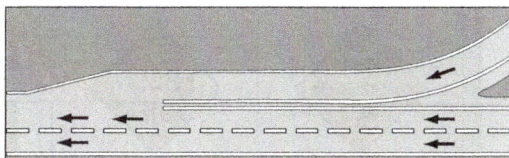

Barrels

Barrels that are engineered to act as an impact cushion reduce the seriousness of crashes. These barrels are usually installed in front of a solid obstacle and in areas of high crash frequency.

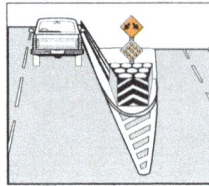

Hearing Impaired

If you see this flag on the back of a bicycle, slow down, as the bicycle operator may be hearing impaired. This sign may also be displayed on vehicles to alert others the driver may be hearing impaired.

Construction and Maintenance Devices

Various traffic control devices are used in construction and maintenance work areas to direct drivers, bicyclists, or pedestrians safely through the work zone and to provide for the safety of the workers.

The most commonly used traffic control devices are signs, barricades, vertical panels, drums, cones, tubes, flashing arrow panels, and flag individuals. Orange is the basic color for these devices.

Special Note: Traffic fines double for violations that occur in construction zones where workers are present.

When you are in a construction and maintenance work area, be prepared:

1. To slow down or stop as you approach workers and equipment

2. To change lanes

3. For unexpected movements of workers and equipment

Construction and Maintenance Signs

Construction and maintenance signs are used to alert drivers of unusual or potentially dangerous conditions in or near work areas. Most signs in work areas are diamond shaped, but a few are rectangular.

Table 21: Construction and Maintenance Signs

Sign	Sign	Sign	Sign
SHOULDER WORK	ROAD CLOSED 1000 FT	DETOUR 1000 FT	END CONSTRUCTION
ONE LANE ROAD 1000 FT	NARROW LANES AHEAD	ROAD WORK 1 MILE	SLOW TRAFFIC AHEAD
(flagger) 500 FEET	ROAD CONSTRUCTION AHEAD	FRESH OIL	DETOUR / ←DETOUR

Channelizing Devices

Barricades, vertical panels, drums, cones, and tubes are the most commonly used devices to alert drivers of unusual or potentially dangerous conditions in highway and street work areas, and to guide drivers safely through the work zone. At night channelizing devices are often equipped with flashing or steady burn lights.

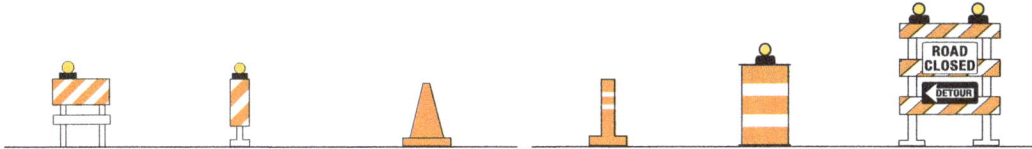

When you encounter any type of channelizing device:

1. Slow down and prepare to change lanes when it is safe to do so.

2. Be prepared for drivers who wait until the last second to move to the open lane.

3. Maintain reduced speed until you clear the construction area. There should be a sign indicating you are leaving the construction area.

4. Return to the normal driving lane only after checking traffic behind you.

Passing Traffic

The diagonal stripes on the barricade or vertical panel guide the driver towards the direction to where the traffic is to pass.

Pass to the Right
Stripes sloping downward to the right means the driver should bear to the right.

Pass to the Left
Stripes sloping downward to the left means the driver should bear to the left.

Flashing Arrow Panels

Large flashing or sequencing arrow panels may be used in work zones day and night to guide drivers into certain traffic lanes and to inform them part of the road ahead is closed.

Flag Person

A flag person is often provided in roadway work zones to stop, slow, or guide traffic safely through the area. A flag person wears an orange vest, shirt, or jacket and uses stop/slow paddles or red flags to direct traffic through work zones.

1. A flag person is used in cases of extreme hazard.

2. A flag person's instructions must be obeyed.

3. When instructed to stop, do so in your lane and do not veer right or left.

4. Do not attempt to go forward until the flag person instructs you to do so.

5. Proceed with caution, expect the unexpected.

6. Always be on the lookout for oncoming vehicles in your lane of traffic.

Automated Flagger Assistance Device (AFAD)

An automated flagger assistance device (AFAD) is used to control road users through temporary traffic zones. An AFAD is designed to be remotely operated, allowing a flag person to be positioned out of the lane of traffic. Temporary traffic control in roadway work zones can also include pilot/escort vehicles, advanced warning signs, or temporary traffic signals.

Obey Warning Signs and Barricades

It is a violation to disobey the instructions, signals, warnings, or markings of a warning sign, or to drive around a barricade.

The offense is a misdemeanor punishable by a fine of $1 to $200. Fines double in a construction or maintenance work zone when workers are present anywhere in the construction zone.

The offense is a Class B misdemeanor punishable by a fine of up to $2,000 and/or up to 180 days in jail when a warning sign or barricade has been placed at a location where water is over any portion of a road, street, or highway.

Slow-Moving Vehicle Emblem

This emblem is required for all slow-moving vehicles. Slow-moving vehicles are those designed to operate at a maximum speed of 25 mph or less, and the term includes all vehicles, farm and other machinery, and any other road machinery drawn by either animals or slow moving motor vehicles.

a. The use of this emblem is prohibited on anything other than a slow-moving vehicle. It must not be used on other vehicles or on stationary objects.

b. Exceptions. The following do not need the special emblem:

1) A vehicle being used in actual construction work while traveling within the limits of a construction area marked as required by the Texas Transportation Commission;

2) An implement or machinery being towed by a slow-moving vehicle bearing an emblem, if this emblem remains visible.

REAR

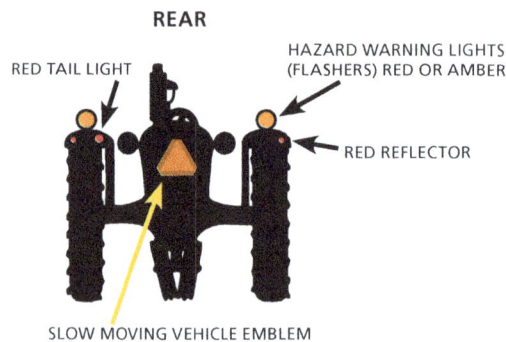

RED TAIL LIGHT

HAZARD WARNING LIGHTS (FLASHERS) RED OR AMBER

RED REFLECTOR

SLOW MOVING VEHICLE EMBLEM

Image source: Some images in this chapter are courtesy of The MUTCD, 2009 Edition, published by FHWA at mutcd.fhwa.dot.gov/pdfs/2009/pdf_index.htm

Chapter 6: Signaling, Passing, and Turning

Signaling

A good driver always lets others know if he/she is going to turn or stop. Signaling communicates your intention when driving and helps other drivers around you to plan ahead. A surprise move often results in a crash. Always be alert, watch for others, and give signals for your movements.

Always signal when you are going to:

1. Change lanes

2. Make a turn

3. Pull away from a parking space parallel to the curb

4. Slow down or stop

5. Enter or leave a highway

6. Pull over to the side of the road

How to Signal

You may either use turn signal lights or hand and arm signals. If using hand signals, extend your hand and arm well out of the car window as shown below. Always make sure your signals can be easily seen by others, and signal in plenty of time.

Hand and arm signals are usually difficult to see during non-daylight hours, so it is important to make sure your signal lights are working properly. When signaling a stop, pump your brakes a few times to attract attention.

Signal continuously for at least 100 feet before turning or stopping, and be sure to turn off your signal lights once your turn is complete. Your unintended signal still means "turn" to other drivers.

Left Turn   Right Turn   Stop or Slow Down

Passing

Keep to the Right

Never drive on the left side of the road when:

1. Pavement markings or signs prohibit driving on the left (a "No Passing Zone" or solid lane lines)

2. There are two or more traffic lanes in each direction

3. Within 100 feet of or crossing an intersection or railroad crossing

4. On a hill, curve, or any other place where vision is limited

5. Within 100 feet of a bridge, viaduct, or tunnel

Always keep to the right side of the road except when:

1. Passing another vehicle on a two- or three-lane street

2. Driving on a one-way street

3. The right side of the road is blocked

Basic Safety Rules When You Are Passing

It is not always safe to pass. Be patient and wait until the time is right. Crashes resulting from improper passing often result in head on crashes and can be deadly.

1. Make certain the way is clear.

2. Give the proper signal before changing lanes.

3. Tap your horn when necessary to avoid surprising the driver ahead.

4. Avoid cutting in too quickly if you must return to your original lane.

LEFT
LANE
FOR
PASSING
ONLY

How to Pass on a Two-Lane Road

1. Keep enough distance between you and the car in front of you so you can see ahead clearly. Check the rearview mirror, your side mirrors, and look over your shoulder in your blind spot to make sure the roadway is clear and no other vehicles are passing you. Turn on your left turn signal to alert any drivers behind you.

2. Check well ahead for signs and pavement markings for no passing zones, and always check for oncoming traffic in the left lane. Be sure you have enough time and space to overtake the car ahead and return to the right lane before an approaching car comes within 200 feet of you.

3. Tap your horn when necessary to alert the driver ahead.

4. Pass on the left and do not return to the right lane until you have safely cleared the overtaken vehicle. Wait until you can see the car you have just passed in your rearview mirror before returning to the right lane.

5. Turn on your right turn signal and return to the right lane. Be sure to turn your signal off after you have completed the lane change.

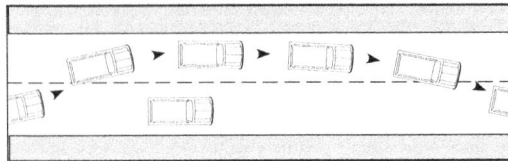

Passing on the Right

In Texas, you can pass on the right only when conditions permit you to do so safely.

1. The road is clear of parked vehicles or other lane obstructions and is wide enough for two or more lanes in each direction.

2. You are on a one-way road.

3. You may pass on a paved shoulder when the vehicle you are passing is slowing or stopped on the main traveled portion of the highway, disabled, or preparing to make a left turn.

Do not pass on the right by driving off the paved portion of the highway.

When Another Vehicle is Passing

1. Do not increase your speed.

2. Stay in your lane.

3. Safely move as far to the right as you can when being passed on the left and the lanes are not marked.

4. Make it as safe and easy as possible for the other driver to pass you.

Blind Spot Driving

When you are passing, do not drive or linger in the other driver's blind spot. Either pass the other driver or slow down so you are not in another driver's blind spot. It is likely the other driver cannot see you if you are in or near their blind spot.

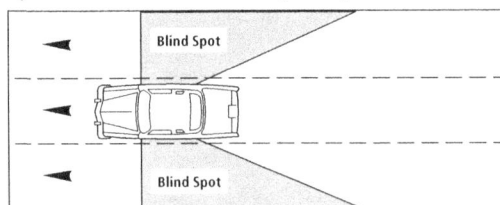

Turning

Turning a corner appears to be a simple operation. However, many crashes and confusion in traffic are caused by drivers who do not turn properly.

Refer to the diagrams showing the correct method of making right and left turns. There are seven steps in making a safe turn.

1. Decide before you get to the turning point. Never make a last minute turn; it is dangerous.

2. Look behind and to both sides to see where other vehicles are before you change lanes.

3. Move into the proper lane as soon as possible. The faster the traffic is moving, the sooner you should move into the proper lane. If you cannot get into the proper lane within one-half block before turning, do not turn, and continue straight ahead.

4. Give the proper turn signal at least 100 feet before you turn. If using a hand signal, hold the signal until you are close enough to the intersection for others to know your intention. Do not hold the signal while making the turn; you need both hands on the wheel.

5. Slow down to a reasonable turning speed prior to making the turn. Don't use the brake or clutch while turning.

6. To properly execute the turn, stay in the proper turn lane at all times. Make the turn correctly. This will be easy if you are in the proper lane and proceeding slowly enough at the time you begin to turn.

7. Finish the turn in the proper lane.

How to Make a Right Turn

1. Signal for a lane change well ahead of the turning point. When it is safe, move your vehicle to the far right lane.

2. Use your right turn signal and slow down at least 100 feet from the corner.

3. Look both ways before starting to turn.

4. Keep as close as possible to the right edge of the road.

5. Turn using both hands on the wheel.

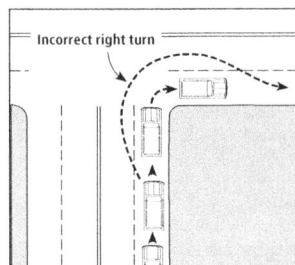

How to Make a Left Turn

1. Well ahead of the turning point, signal for a lane change. When it is safe, move into the center lane.

2. Use the left turn signal and slow down at least 100 feet from the corner.

3. Look in all directions before starting to turn. Stay to the right of the center line as you enter the intersection. Yield the right-of-way to any vehicle approaching from the opposite direction.

4. To complete a left turn you should turn to the right of the center line of the road into which you are turning by entering the lane in which you will interfere the least with other traffic.

5. Once you have completed your left turn, you may signal and change lanes if necessary.

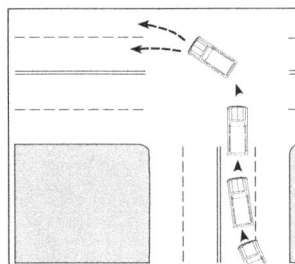

Making a Left Turn From a One-Way Onto a Two-Way Street

If you are turning left from a one-way street you should turn from the left lane into the right lane, moving in the same direction.

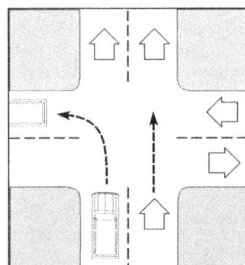

Making a Left Turn From a Two-Way Onto a One-Way Street

If you are turning left onto a one-way street, enter the street in the lane in which you will interfere the least with other traffic.

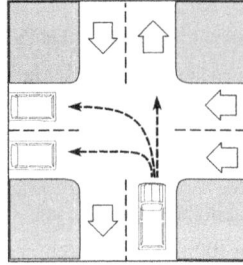

Other Turning Procedures

Watch for pavement markings and signs that:

1. Permit turning right or left from or into two or more traffic lanes

2. Give other special turning or lane information

Chapter 7: Parking, Stopping, or Standing

Not all crashes happen while a vehicle is moving. An improperly parked vehicle may also cause a crash. When you leave your vehicle, turn the motor off, set the parking brake and remove the key. Be sure to look behind you for any oncoming traffic before opening your car door.

Do Not Park, Stop, or Stand a Vehicle

In the following situations, you should not park, stop, or allow a vehicle to stand idling:

1. On the road side of any vehicle stopped or parked at the edge or curb of a street

2. On a sidewalk or crosswalk

3. Within an intersection

4. Between a safety zone and adjacent curb or within 30 feet of a place on the curb immediately opposite the end of a safety zone

5. Alongside or opposite of any street excavation or obstruction when stopping, standing, or parking would obstruct traffic

6. On a bridge or other elevated structure on a highway or within a highway tunnel

7. On any railroad track

8. At any place where an official sign prohibits stopping

Do Not Park or Stand a Vehicle

Whether occupied or not, do not park or allow a vehicle to stand idling:

1. In front of a public or private driveway

2. Within 15 feet of a fire hydrant

3. Within 20 feet of a crosswalk at an intersection

4. Within 30 feet upon the approach to any flashing signal, stop sign, yield sign, or other traffic control signal located at the side of a road

5. Within 20 feet of the driveway entrance to any fire station and on the side of a street opposite the entrance to any fire station within 75 feet of entrance

6. At any place where an official sign prohibits parking or standing

Special Note: Temporarily stopping to obey signs, signals, etc. is not considered parking or standing.

Do Not Park a Vehicle

1. Do not park a vehicle, occupied or not, within 50 feet of the nearest rail of a railroad crossing.

2. Do not park a vehicle at any place where an official sign prohibits parking.

Parking, Stopping, or Standing on a Highway Outside an Urban Area

Never park or leave a vehicle to stand idling on the paved part of any highway outside of a business or residential district when you can park off the road. If you cannot park off the road:

1. Leave plenty of room for others to pass

2. Be sure your vehicle can be seen for at least 200 feet from each direction

3. If at night, use your parking lights or leave your headlights on dim

4. A person may stop, stand, or park a bicycle on a sidewalk if the bicycle does not impede the normal and reasonable movement of pedestrian or other traffic on the sidewalk.

Disabled Parking

It is a violation for a person to park, stand, or stop a vehicle in a parking space designated as disabled parking. Illegally parking in a space reserved for individuals with disabilities is a misdemeanor punishable by a fine of $500 to $750 for the first offense. This fine increases with additional offenses up to $1,250 for five or more offenses. Additional offenses also include community service.

Texas law specifically states:

1. You may not park in a disabled parking space unless the vehicle has a disabled license plate or state issued removable windshield identification card.

2. You may not use a disabled parking windshield identification card unless transporting the disabled person to whom it was issued.

3. You may not lend your windshield identification card to someone else.

4. You may not block an access or curb ramp.

5. You may not make, sell, possess, or display a counterfeit disabled parking windshield identification card, or alter a disabled parking windshield identification card.

Certain municipalities also prohibit stopping or standing in a disabled parking space unless a disabled parking windshield identification card is visible or the vehicle has a disabled license plate.

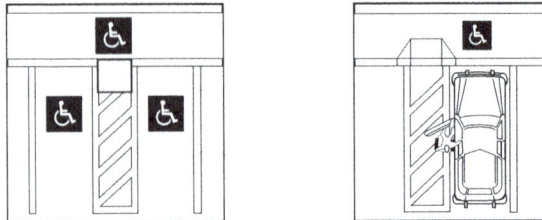

Do not park in striped areas adjacent to disabled parking spaces or in a striped area in front of an entrance to a business adjacent to a disabled parking space. Striped areas are for wheelchair lifts.

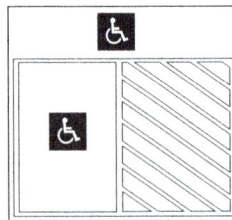

Unattended Motor Vehicle

It is illegal for any driver to permit their car to stand idling unattended without turning off the engine, locking the ignition, removing the key from the ignition, and setting the brake; and when standing on any grade, without turning the front wheels to the curb or side of the road.

The requirements regarding turning off the engine, locking the ignition, and removing the key do not apply to a driver who starts the engine by using a remote starter or other similar device that remotely starts the engine without the key in the ignition. Before the vehicle can be operated, the key must be placed in the ignition or must be physically present in the vehicle.

Parallel Parking

1. Choose a space large enough for your car to fit. Signal then stop even with the front of the car about two feet out from the space. To alert drivers who may be behind you be sure to signal before you pass the spot you want to parallel park in.

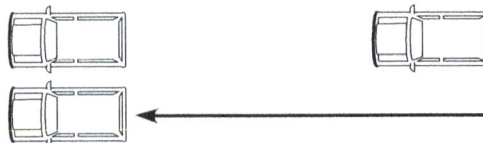

2. Make sure you will not interfere with oncoming traffic then turn your front wheels all the way to the right and back slowly toward the curb.

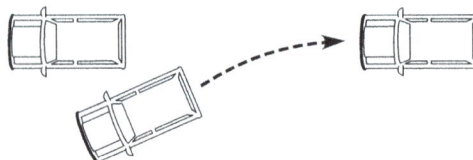

Special Note:
On a roadway that allows two-way traffic, the driver must park with the vehicle's right-hand wheels within 18 inches of the right-hand curb or edge of the roadway.

3. When your front seat is opposite the rear bumper of the car ahead, turn your steering wheel all the way to the left. Back slowly toward the car behind you without touching it. You should be about six inches from the curb. Do not park more than 18 inches from the curb or edge of the road.

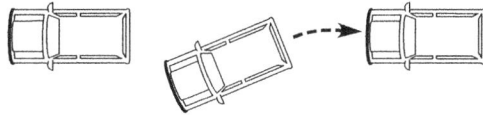

4. Straighten your front wheels and pull into the final parking position. Center your car in the space.

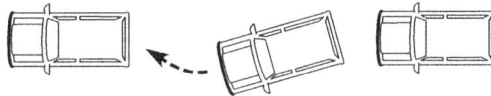

Parking on Hills

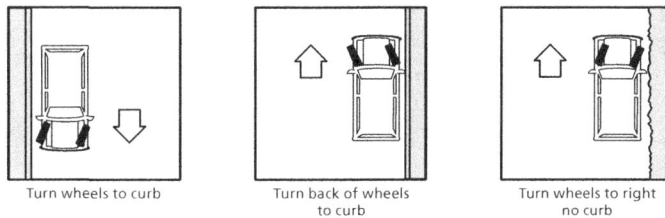

| Turn wheels to curb | Turn back of wheels to curb | Turn wheels to right no curb |

Leaving a Parking Space

Use caution when leaving any parking space and check all of your mirrors to make sure nothing is obstructing your vehicle's path, especially pedestrians or children. Children often play between parked cars. Look back before and while you're backing up. Be sure to use your signal to notify other drivers you are leaving your current parking spot.

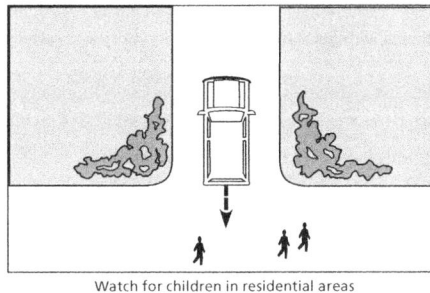

Watch for children in residential areas

Coasting

It is illegal to coast on a downgrade with the gears or transmission in neutral.

Chapter 8: Speed and Speed Limits

Speed

Generally, you should drive at the same speed as the main stream of traffic and always be aware of how fast you are traveling. You must always obey the speed limit and you should consider these best practices below:

Special Note: When the vehicle ahead of you passes a fixed object and you reach the same fixed object in less than two seconds, you are following too closely.

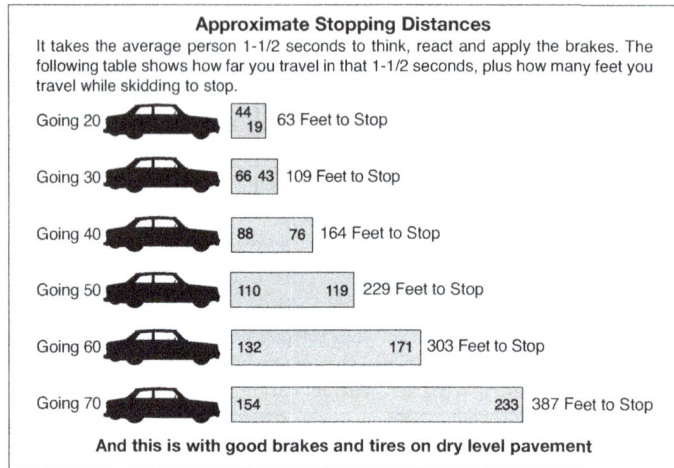

1. You should keep a safe distance between your car and the one in front of you. The faster you drive, the greater the distance you should keep from the car ahead of you. For speeds 30 mph or less, the minimum time between your car and the one in front of you is 2 seconds with good road conditions. For speeds above 30 mph, maintain a 4 second gap between cars during good road conditions. During periods of poor road conditions, allow more time. Using a four-second following interval is the best practice for a beginning or less experienced driver.

Approximate Stopping Distances

It takes the average person 1-1/2 seconds to think, react and apply the brakes. The following table shows how far you travel in that 1-1/2 seconds, plus how many feet you travel while skidding to stop.

Going 20	44 / 19	63 Feet to Stop
Going 30	66 43	109 Feet to Stop
Going 40	88 76	164 Feet to Stop
Going 50	110 119	229 Feet to Stop
Going 60	132 171	303 Feet to Stop
Going 70	154 233	387 Feet to Stop

And this is with good brakes and tires on dry level pavement

2. You should adjust your speed and following distance according to your physical condition and the conditions of the vehicle and road. If you are tired or not feeling well, do not drive. Never force yourself to drive.

3. You should know when to slow down and increase the following distance.

   a. Slow down and increase the following distance when the road is wet. Many drivers find out too late what a small amount of rain can do. Roads become slippery when wet, making your car harder to control. Slow down and make sure you have complete control of the situation at all times.

   b. Slow down and increase the following distance when the road is crowded.

   c. Slow down and increase the following distance when your vision is limited. You should always be able to stop within the distance you can see ahead of your car. In the dark or in bad weather, do not over-drive your range of vision.

Speed Reduces Your Field of Vision

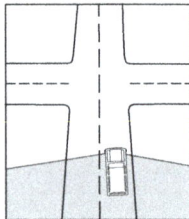

Stationary	**20 MPH**	**40 MPH**	**60 MPH**
Field of vision is 180 degrees or more	Field of vision reduced to about 2/3	Field of vision reduced to about 2/5	Field of vision reduced to about 1/5

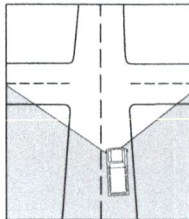

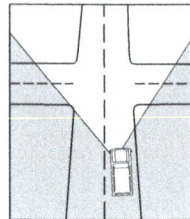

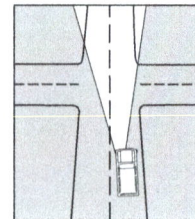

Speed Limits

Drivers are required to obey posted minimum and maximum speed limits. These limits are designed to provide for the orderly flow of traffic under normal driving conditions. During periods of heavy traffic, bad weather, low visibility, or other poor driving conditions, you must adjust your speed and following distance to help avoid crashes.

The *Speed Limits* table shows the maximum speed limits for all vehicles under different conditions. Drivers must also be aware cities and counties have the authority to change these limits. Entities that establish or alter a speed limit must establish the same speed limit for daytime and nighttime.

Table 22: Speed Limits

Type of Roadway	Speed (MPH)
Urban District	30
Alley	15
Beaches and County Roads adjacent to a public beach (if declared by the commissioners court of the county)	15
Highway numbered by Texas or the U.S. outside an urban district including Farm to Market and Ranch to Market roads Passenger cars, motorcycles, light truck, passenger car or light truck towing a trailer or semi-trailer, truck or truck-tractor, truck or truck-tractor towing a trailer or semi-trailer, buses, school activity bus.	70
School Buses which have passed a commercial vehicle inspection.	60
Highway not numbered by Texas or the U.S. and outside an urban district: Passenger cars, motorcycles, light truck, passenger car or light truck towing a trailer or semi-trailer, truck or truck-tractor, truck or truck-tractor towing a trailer or semi-trailer, buses, school activity bus.	60
School buses that have not passed a commercial vehicle inspection or are traveling on a highway not numbered by Texas or the U.S.	50

The Texas Transportation Commission, regional mobility authorities and local governments have authority to raise or lower speed limits based on traffic studies and other statutory requirements. Many limited access highways have speed limits of 75 up to 85 mph. Always be aware of and observe the posted speed limit for the roadway on which you are driving.

Slow Down or Move Over

If an emergency medical vehicle, law enforcement vehicle, fire truck, tow truck, utility service vehicle, Texas Department of Transportation vehicle (TxDOT, or other highway construction or maintenance vehicle) is stopped on the road with its lights activated (the lights are on or flashing), then the driver is required:

1. To reduce his/her speed to 20 mph below the speed limit; or

2. Move out of the lane closest to the emergency medical vehicle, law enforcement vehicle, fire truck, tow truck or a TxDOT vehicle if the road has multiple lanes traveling in the same direction.

There are other instances where it is important to be observant of vehicles stopped on the road. Mail, delivery, and trash-collection vehicles often make frequent stops in the roadway. Drivers must proceed with caution, and, if possible, change lanes before safely passing one of these vehicles on the road.

Street Racing

Street racing, also known as drag racing, is illegal and can result in serious injuries or fatalities. Illegal street racers put other drivers at risk because races are typically held on public roads. Due to the high speeds, drivers are unable to react to common road hazards or other driving situations, which often results in crashes.

Illegal street racing also causes unnecessary property damage, including extensive wear on roads (due to the high-powered engines damaging asphalt), which requires costly repairs at the expense to the tax-payer.

Please visit the National Highway Traffic Safety Administration (NHTSA) https://www.nhtsa.gov/risky-driving/speeding for speed related fatalities.

A person may not participate in:

1. A race;

2. A vehicle speed competition or contest;

3. A drag race or acceleration contest;

4. A test of physical endurance of the operator of a vehicle; or

5. In connection with a drag race, an exhibition of vehicle speed or acceleration, or to make a speed record.

The criminal penalty for a conviction of Speed Racing ranges from a Class B misdemeanor to a second-degree felony.

Chapter 9: Some Special Driving Situations

Driving at night is much more dangerous than driving during the day. Many people do not see as well at night. When taking a trip, it is safer to drive during daylight hours. Also, never drive when you are tired.

Headlights

Slow down when driving at night and be sure you can stop within the distance lit by your headlights.

You must use your headlights beginning 30 minutes after sunset and ending 30 minutes before sunrise, or anytime when individuals or vehicles cannot be seen clearly for at least 1,000 feet.

Avoid looking directly into the headlights of approaching vehicles; shift your eyes down to the lower right side of your traffic lane.

Use your low beam headlights when:

1. Within 500 feet of an approaching vehicle

2. Following closely (within 300 feet) behind another vehicle

3. Driving on lighted roads

4. Driving in fog, heavy rain, sleet, snow, or dust

If you must park on an unlighted highway at night, leave your parking lights or low beam headlights on.

Highway Driving

Freeways, toll-roads, throughways, turnpikes, and expressways are designed for maximum safety, but you must know how to use them properly. In Texas, a highway is defined as the width between the boundary lines of a publicly maintained way, any part of which is open to the public for vehicular travel.

Before Using a Highway

Plan your trip in advance so you know your entrance, direction, and exit. Make sure you and your car are in good condition. If you cannot or do not want to drive at or above the minimum speed limit, do not use the highway.

Entering the Highway

1. You must yield the right-of-way to vehicles already on the highway.

2. Enter the speed change lane, stay to the right, signal left, and when it is clear, increase your speed to merge with the flow of traffic.

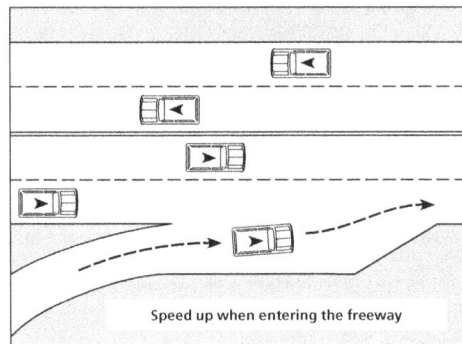

Speed up when entering the freeway

Driving on the Highway

Choose the Proper Lane

1. Use the right lane to drive at the minimum posted speed limit or below the normal flow of traffic.

2. Use the middle or left lane if you are traveling faster than other traffic or passing other vehicles.

3. If you plan to leave the freeway soon, change to the exit lane as soon as possible.

Observe Specific Instructions
Observe specific instructions indicating the lane you should drive in.

Once You are in the Proper Lane

1. Stay in the middle of your lane.

2. Do not weave in and out of traffic.

3. Maintain a constant speed. Keep pace with the traffic. Don't speed up and slow down unnecessarily.

4. Stay at least two seconds behind the vehicle ahead of you. In bad weather, increase the time to at least four seconds. Watch the cars ahead of you. Be prepared if one of the cars ahead of you stops suddenly.

5. Adjust your speed to allow others to enter the highway safely.

6. Vehicles in any lane, except the right lane used for slower traffic, should be prepared to move to another lane to allow faster traffic to pass.

Leaving the Highway

1. Move into the proper lane well in advance of the exit. The greater the amount of traffic, the earlier you should move into the proper lane. Exit signs are usually placed at least 1,000 yards ahead of the exit.

2. Slow down on the exit ramp so by the time you are off the highway, you are within the new, slower speed limit.

Fight Highway Hypnosis
A condition of drowsiness or unawareness can be brought on by reduced activity and steady sounds of wind, engine, and tire hum. This is known as highway hypnosis. All drivers should be aware of its danger and of the methods for fighting it.

1. Stop often. Even if you are feeling well, you should stop at least every two hours or every 100 miles. Get out of your car and walk around. Allow your muscles to relax.

2. Do not drive more than eight hours per day.

3. Keep shifting your eyes. Look at different objects; near and far, left and right. Read the road signs as you approach them. Check your rearview mirror.

Highway Safety Tips

1. Keep a window open so there is always fresh air in the car to help keep you alert and awake.

2. On bright days, wear good sunglasses. Never wear sunglasses at night.

3. Stay out of another driver's blind spot. Traveling where the driver ahead of you cannot see your vehicle can be dangerous. Stay behind or go around the other vehicle. Do not follow to the side.

4. Avoid using a cell phone while driving; use may cause distraction and driver inattention. If you must use a cell phone, safely pull off the road or use a hands-free headset. If you are under 18 years of age, it is illegal to use a cell phone while driving even if it is a hands-free device except in the case of emergency.

Vehicle Breakdown

1. If you can't get the car off the road, get everyone out of the car and off the road. Portable warning devices should be used to warn oncoming traffic.

2. Move your car off the pavement to the side of the road. A car with a flat tire or blowout can be driven slowly off the road.

3. Turn on your emergency warning lights. If you do not have warning lights, use your taillights. At night, in addition to your taillights and warning lights, turn the lights on inside of the car.

4. Tie a white cloth to your radio antenna, door handle, or some other place where it may be easily seen. If you do not have a white cloth, raise your hood.

Controlling a Car in Special Situations
There is one basic rule which applies in all driving situations, **think** before you **act**.

Steering Out of a Skid
An automobile skids when its tires lose their grip on the road surface. If the car starts to skid, follow these safety tips.

1. Do not hit the brakes suddenly and hard. Take your foot off the gas pedal (accelerator).

2. Turn your steering wheel in the direction of the skid. As you recover control, gently straighten the wheels.

3. Avoid a situation that could cause a skid by slowing down when the road and weather conditions are poor. Also, check your car's tires. Old or worn tires that have minimal or damaged tread are dangerous. (In the illustration below, the direction of the skid is to the right.)

Steering out of a skid

Turn steering wheel in
direction of skid

Brake Failure

If your car brakes fail, do not panic. Remember you can use your parking brake and shift to a lower gear. Apply your parking brake cautiously to keep from locking the brakes and throwing your car into a skid.

Running Off the Pavement

If something causes you to swerve and run off the pavement:

- Do not hit the brakes suddenly and hard. Grip the steering wheel tightly and take your foot off the gas pedal.

- Use your brakes carefully and do not swing back onto the pavement. Wait until your speed is reduced, check the traffic behind you, and then carefully drive back onto the pavement.

Flat Tire or Blowout

If you have a flat tire or a blowout:

- Do not hit the brakes suddenly and hard

- Take your foot off the gas pedal and gently apply the brakes

- Steer straight ahead to a stop

Driving Down a Steep Hill

When driving down a steep hill, you can shift your car into a low gear to help slow your vehicle. Never coast in neutral or for cars with a standard transmission, never coast with your foot on the clutch.

Winter Driving

Most drivers realize winter creates additional hazards, but many drivers don't know what to do about it. Here are a few precautions you should follow during winter.

Table 23: Winter Driving Safety Tips

Safety Tip	Explanation
Maintain a safe interval	Increase the distance from the vehicle ahead of you according to the conditions of the pavement. Many rear-end collisions occur on icy streets because drivers don't leave space to stop. Snow tires will slide on ice or packed snow. To keep safe, you must keep your distance.
Reduce speed to correspond with conditions	There is no such thing as a "safe" speed range at which you may drive on snow or ice. You must be extremely cautious until you are able to determine how much traction you can expect from your tires. Avoid locking of brakes on ice as it will cause a loss of steering and control. Every city block and every mile of highway may be different, depending upon sun or shade and the surface of the road.
Keep windows clear	Remove snow and ice before you drive, even if you're just driving a few miles. Make certain the windshield wipers and defroster are working properly.
Watch for danger spots ahead	There may be ice on bridges when the rest of the pavement is clear. Snow melts more slowly in shady areas. Take precautions when approaching turns.
Get a feel for the road	Start out very slowly. It is useless to burn the rubber off your tires by spinning the wheels. Test your brakes gently after the car is in motion to determine how much traction you have. Start slowing down before you come to a turn.
Equip your vehicle with chains or snow tires	Chains are the most effective and should be used where ice and snow remain on the road. One word of caution, neither chains nor snow tires will permit you to drive on slick pavement at normal speeds so don't get a false feeling of security.

Roundabouts

Modern Roundabout

A modern roundabout is a one-way, circular intersection where traffic flows counter clockwise around a center island. Modern roundabouts use yield signs rather than traffic lights to control vehicles entering the intersection. This intersection design only has eight potential conflict points, opposed to a traditional "four-way" signalized intersection which has 32 potential conflict points.

Driving in a Modern Roundabout

Road signs, pavement markings and its design help guide drivers through a modern roundabout.

To drive in a modern roundabout, follow these simple steps: slow down as you approach the intersection, yield to traffic already in the circle, enter the circle and follow the loop in a counter clockwise direction, and then make a right turn to exit the roundabout.

There are two types of modern roundabouts: single-lane roundabouts and multi-lane roundabouts.

Single-lane roundabout: Slow down as you approach the roundabout intersection and observe any posted advisory speed signs.

Modern roundabouts reduce severe crashes at intersections by an average of 80%.

FHWA-SA-17-055

Image source: US Department of Transportation - Federal Highway Administration

Yield to traffic driving in the circle. When there is an acceptable gap, enter the circle and travel counterclockwise around the circle. Make a right turn by using your turn signal when exiting the circle.

Observe traffic signs and pavement markings when navigating a roundabout. Also, look for bicyclists and pedestrians using the crosswalks on the roundabout approaches and exits.

Multi-lane roundabouts: Go through the same steps as a single-lane roundabout and follow these additional steps. When approaching a multi-lane roundabout, observe the advance lane movement sign for choosing the correct entry lane. Also, do not change lanes while driving in the circle.

When navigating all roundabouts, give space for large vehicles, such as semitrailers, buses, and fire trucks that need more than one lane when driving around the circle. Also, pull over for emergency vehicles on the roundabout approaches and exits. However, do not stop for emergency vehicles in the roundabout circle. Clear the circle first and then pull over for the emergency vehicle.

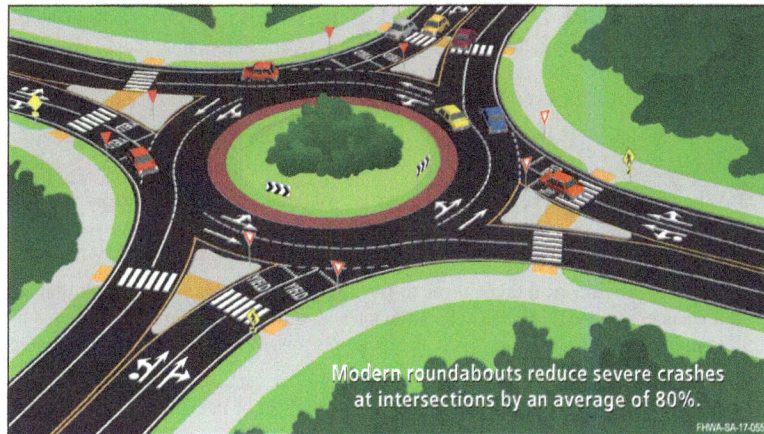

Floods

Floods are one of the most common hazards in the U.S. Nearly half of all flash flood fatalities are vehicle-related.

These are the facts:

- Six inches of water will reach the bottom of most passenger cars, causing loss of control and possible stalling.

- Twelve inches of water will float many cars.

- Two feet of rushing water will carry away pick-up trucks, SUVs, and most other vehicles.

- Water across a road may hide a missing segment of roadbed or a missing bridge. Roads weaken under floodwater and drivers should proceed cautiously after waters have receded since the road may collapse under the vehicle's weight.

National Weather Service and Texas Division of Emergency Management officials say if your vehicle stalls in floodwater, get out quickly and move to higher ground. Better yet, when there's water on the road, Turn Around Don't Drown®. Saving your life is as simple as choosing an alternate route.

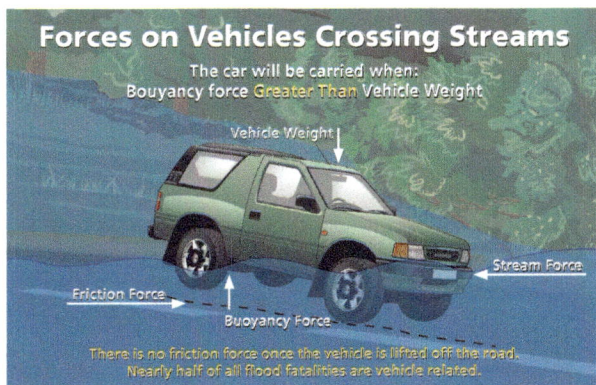

Forces on Vehicles Crossing Streams

The car will be carried when: Bouyancy force Greater Than Vehicle Weight

Vehicle Weight

Friction Force

Stream Force

Buoyancy Force

There is no friction force once the vehicle is lifted off the road. Nearly half of all flood fatalities are vehicle related.

For more information on flood safety, visit the National Weather Service website: https://www.weather.gov/safety/flood.

Turn Around Don't Drown® *(Note: Per National Weather Service any use of Turn Around Don't Drown must include the registration symbol.)*

Share the Road with Trucks (Large trucks and truck-tractor combinations)

Whether you are sharing the road with a passenger car, motorcycle, truck, bus, or other vehicle, it is important to obey traffic laws, abide by the rules of the road, and drive defensively. Trucks are designed to carry products to and from towns and cities; they are designed to be as maneuverable as cars. Trucks have longer stopping and accelerating distances, a wider turning radius, and weigh more.

Passing

1. When passing a truck, first check to your front and rear, check mirrors and blind spots, then move into the passing lane only if it is clear and you are in a legal passing zone. Let the truck driver know you are passing by flashing your headlights, especially at night. The truck driver should make it easier for you to pass by staying to the far side of the lane.

2. On a level highway, it takes three to five seconds longer to pass a truck than a car. On an upgrade, a truck often loses speed so it's easier to pass than a car. On a downgrade, the truck's momentum causes the truck to go faster so you may need to increase your speed. Complete your pass as quickly as possible and don't stay alongside the other vehicle.

3. If the driver flashes the truck's lights after you pass, it's a signal that it is clear for you to pull back in front of the truck. Be sure to move back only when you can see the entire front of the truck in your rearview mirror. After you pass a truck, maintain your speed.

4. When a truck passes you, help the truck driver by keeping to the far side of your lane. You'll make it easier for the truck driver if you slightly reduce your speed. Don't speed up while the truck is passing. After passing, the truck driver should signal to let you know he is returning to your lane.

5. When you meet a truck coming from the opposite direction, keep as far to the side as possible to avoid a sideswipe crash and to reduce the wind turbulence between the two vehicles. Remember, turbulence pushes vehicles apart; it does not pull them together.

Following a Truck

1. Tractor-trailers take longer to stop than a car traveling at the same speed. The average passenger car traveling at 55 mph can stop in approximately 240 feet, which is about three-fourths the length of a football field. A fully loaded tractor-trailer may take more than 400 feet to completely stop, well over the length of a football field.

2. If you're following a truck, stay out of its blind spot at the rear. The blind spot is the area behind the truck that the driver cannot see in his rearview mirrors. Avoid following too closely, and position your vehicle so the truck driver can see your vehicle in the truck's side view mirror. An excellent rule of thumb for motorists sharing the road with a tractor-trailer is, "If you can't see the truck driver in his side mirror, he can't see you." By avoiding the truck driver's blind spot, you will have a good view of the road ahead, and the truck driver can give you plenty of warning for a stop or a turn. This will allow you more time to react and make a safe stop.

3. When you follow a truck at night always dim your headlights. Bright lights from a vehicle behind will blind the truck driver when the lights reflect off the truck's large side mirrors.

4. If you are stopped behind a truck on an upgrade, leave space in case the truck drifts back when it starts to move. Also, keep to the left in your lane so the driver can see you're stopped behind the truck.

Right Turns

Pay attention to turn signals. Trucks make wide, right turns and sometimes leave an open space to the right just before the turn. To avoid a crash, don't pass a truck on the right if there is a possibility the truck might make a right turn.

Backing Crashes

Never cross behind a truck preparing to back up. When a truck driver is preparing to back the truck from a road into a loading area, the road is temporarily blocked. Wait for the truck to complete its maneuver before trying to pass. If you pass too closely behind the truck, a crash may occur because you are in the truck's blind spot.

Maneuverability

On multi-lane highways, tractor-trailers stay in the center lane to help the flow of local traffic on and off the highway. Staying in the center lane also increases the truck driver's options if he/she has to switch lanes to avoid a crash. Be aware of common mistakes drivers should avoid when driving around trucks and buses.

Cutting Off a Vehicle to Reach Your Exit or Turn

Never cut in front of a truck. Cutting into the open space in front of a truck or bus removes the driver's cushion of safety. Trying to beat a truck to a single-lane construction zone represents a particularly dangerous situation. Either slow down and exit or stay behind the truck.

Never Underestimate the Size and Speed of an Approaching Tractor-trailer

Because of its large size, a tractor-trailer often appears to be traveling at a slower speed than it is. A substantial number of car and truck collisions take place at intersections because the driver of the car does not realize how close the truck is or how quickly it is approaching.

Share the Road with Motorcycles

Individuals who operate a motorcycle have the same rights and privileges as any other vehicle on the road.

For various reasons, drivers may not see the motorcyclist, and approximately one-half of all motorcycle crashes involve another vehicle. According to the National Highway Traffic Safety Administration, motorcyclists are about 35 times more likely to die in a traffic crash than passenger car occupants. A few of the most common reasons are provided below.

1. Many drivers tend to look for other cars, not for motorcyclists.

2. The profile of a motorcycle is much smaller than the profile of a car, making an approaching motorcyclist harder to see.

3. Estimating the distance and speed of a motorcycle is more difficult than it is for a car.

4. Motorcycle riding requires frequent lane movements to adjust to changing road conditions.

5. Distracted driving, such as texting or talking on a cell phone.

Situations When Crashes Are Most Likely to Occur

Motorcycle crashes are most likely to occur in the high-risk situations described below.

Left Turns

The most common crash between cars and motorcycles is at an intersection when the driver of a car is making a left turn in front of a motorcycle.

A Car's Blind Spot

Motorcyclists are often hidden in a vehicle's blind spot or missed in a quick look due to their smaller size. Always make a visual check for motorcycles by checking mirrors and blind spots before entering or leaving a lane of traffic and at intersections.

Hazardous Road Conditions

Road conditions that are a minor annoyance to you may pose a major hazard to motorcyclists. Motorcyclists may suddenly change speed or adjust their position within a lane in reaction to changes in the weather, road, or traffic conditions. This may include potholes, gravel, railroad crossings, and wet or slippery surfaces which impair the motorcyclists' braking and handling abilities. Expect and allow room for such actions by the motorcyclist.

Strong Winds

A strong gust of wind can move a motorcycle across an entire lane if the rider isn't prepared for it. Wind gusts from large trucks in the other lane can also be a hazard.

Large Vehicles

A large vehicle such as a van, bus, or truck can block a motorcycle from a driver's view and the motorcyclist may seem to suddenly appear from nowhere.

Motorcycle Driving Awareness

Look Out for Motorcyclists

Although you may not see any cars, be aware there may be a motorcycle. Be careful at intersections, and always take a second look for a motorcycle before turning at an intersection, particularly when making left turns.

Signal Your Intentions

Always signal before changing lanes or merging with traffic. This allows the motorcyclist to anticipate traffic flow and find a safe lane position. Signal even if you don't see cars or motorcycles. Be careful when making left turns across lanes of approaching traffic. Look carefully in all directions for approaching motorcyclists. Don't be fooled by a flashing turn signal. Motorcycle signals usually are not self-canceling and riders sometimes forget to turn them off. Wait to be sure the motorcycle is going to turn before you proceed.

Respect a Motorcycle

Allow the motorcyclist a full lane width. Although it may seem as though there is enough room in the traffic lane for an automobile and a motorcycle, the motorcycle is entitled to a full lane and may need the room to maneuver safely. Do not attempt to share the lane with a motorcycle.

Allow Plenty of Space When Following a Motorcycle

The slightest contact can mean a spill or injury for the rider. Allow more following distance, at least four to six seconds, when following a motorcycle so the motorcyclist has enough time to maneuver or stop in an emergency. Stop a safe distance behind the motorcyclist at intersections, signals, or crossings. A full vehicle length is recommended to help prevent impact with the motorcycle should your vehicle suffer a rear end collision. In dry conditions, motorcycles can stop more quickly than a car, so being aware and alert at all times can help prevent a collision.

Special Note: If you drive aware of motorcyclists in these situations, you can help make the streets and roads safer for everyone.

Texas Motorcycle Operator Training Program

The Texas Legislature created the Motorcycle Operator Training and Safety program in 1983 and moved its administration from DPS to TDLR in 2020. The Program's aim is to improve rider skills and reduce the number and severity of motorcycle crashes in Texas. A portion of each motorcycle license fee is used to support this program. The program develops curriculum and monitors motorcycle training classes throughout the state and promotes motorcycle safety and awareness through campaigns, exhibits, and materials.

Contact TDLR at https://www.tdlr.texas.gov/ for more information about motorcycle safety and training courses.

Share the Road with Light Rail

In recent years, light rail has been established in many major cities in Texas. As you travel these areas, you may notice these trains move along the streets just like other vehicles. Light rail is very quiet; and, in fact, quieter than most buses and cars. So whether you are riding a light rail or just walking or driving near the train or tracks, it's important to stay alert and observe the safety rules.

Table 24: Safety Rules for Light Rail

Action	Description
Stop	- Don't walk in front of, between, or behind a train. - Trains can't start or stop quickly regardless of traffic flow. - Do not drive, stop, or park your vehicle on the tracks. It's dangerous and illegal.
Look	- Cross the tracks only at designated crossings and only when it is safe. - Look both ways before crossing the tracks. Trains travel in both directions. - Obey all warning signs, flashing lights, signals, and crossing gates. A law enforcement officer will issue tickets to violators.
Listen	- Stay alert. Light rail is quieter than a bus or most cars. You may not hear a light rail coming. - Listen for train horns and signal bells. - Always follow instructions from a law enforcement officer.
Don't	- Never race a train, run in front of a train, or put anything on or near the tracks. - Never try to beat the train to a crossing. Even in a tie, you lose. - Never drive around crossing gate arms.

Share the Road with Bicycles

A bicycle is a vehicle. Any person riding a bicycle has all of the rights and responsibilities as a driver of a vehicle.

Rules for Motorists and Bicyclists

1. Bicyclists are not restricted to the right lane of traffic. One-way, multi-lane streets are one example of this. Another instance is when the bicyclist is changing lanes to make a left turn. The bicyclists should follow the same path any other vehicle would take traveling in the same direction.

2. A motorist should merge with bicycle traffic when preparing for a right turn. Avoid turning directly across the path of bicycle traffic.

3. Bicyclists are required to ride as far to the right in the lane as possible only when the lane can be shared safely by a car and a bicycle, side-by-side. Even then, there are certain conditions that allow a bicyclist to take the full lane.

   a. The bicyclist is overtaking and passing another, vehicle proceeding in the same direction.

   b. The bicyclist is preparing for a left turn at an intersection or onto a private road or driveway.

   c. There are unsafe conditions in the road, such as fixed or moving objects, parked or moving vehicles, pedestrians, animals, potholes, or debris.

   d. The lane is of substandard width, making it unsafe for a car and a bicycle to safely share the lane side-by-side. When this is the case, it is best for the cyclist to take the full lane, whether riding single file or two abreast.

Car-Bicycle Crashes

Be on the lookout for cyclists on the road, especially at intersections. The most common car-bicycle crashes caused by a motorist are:

1. A motorist turns left in front of oncoming bicycle traffic. Oncoming bicycle traffic is often overlooked or its speed misjudged.

2. A motorist turns right across the path of the bicycle. The motorist should slow down and merge with the bicycle traffic for a safe right turn.

3. A motorist pulls away from a stop sign and fails to yield the right-of-way to bicycle cross traffic. At intersections, the right-of-way rules apply equally to motor vehicles and bicycles.

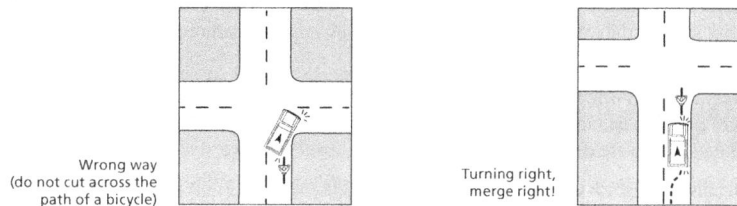

Wrong way
(do not cut across the
path of a bicycle)

Turning right,
merge right!

Image source: Some images in this chapter are courtesy of The MUTCD, 2009 Edition, published by FHWA at mutcd.fhwa.dot.gov/pdfs/2009/pdf_index.htm

Distracted driving

Whenever you are driving a vehicle and your attention is not on the road, you're putting yourself, your passengers, other vehicles, and pedestrians in danger. Distracted driving can result when you perform any activity that may shift your full attention from the driving task. Taking your eyes off the road or hands off the steering wheel presents obvious driving risks. Mental activities that take your mind away from driving are just as dangerous. Your eyes can gaze at objects in the driving scene but fail to see them because your attention is distracted elsewhere.

Activities that can distract your attention include texting, talking to passengers, adjusting the radio, CD player or climate controls; eating, drinking or smoking; reading maps or other literature; picking up something that fell; reading billboards and other road advertisements; watching other people and vehicles including aggressive drivers; talking and/or texting on a cell phone or CB radio; using telematics devices (such as navigation systems, pagers, etc.); daydreaming or being occupied with other mental distractions.

If drivers react a half-second slower because of distractions, crashes double. Some tips to follow so you won't become distracted:

- Review and be totally familiar with all safety and usage features on any in-vehicle electronics, including your wireless device or cell phone, before you drive.
- Pre-program radio stations.
- Pre-load your favorite CDs or cassette tapes.
- Clear the vehicle of any unnecessary objects.
- Review maps and plan your route before you begin driving.
- Adjust all mirrors for the best all-round visibility before you start your trip.
- Do not attempt to read, text, or write while you drive.
- Avoid smoking, eating and drinking while you drive.
- Don't engage in complex or emotionally intense conversations with other occupants.

You need to be able to recognize other drivers who are engaged in any form of driving distraction. Not recognizing other distracted drivers can prevent you from perceiving or reacting correctly in time to prevent a crash. Watch for:

- Vehicles that may drift over the lane divider lines or within their own lane.
- Vehicles traveling at inconsistent speeds.
- Drivers who are preoccupied with maps, food, cigarettes, cell phones, or other objects.
- Drivers who appear to be involved in conversations with their passengers.

Give a distracted driver plenty of room and maintain your safe following distance.

Be very careful when passing a driver who seems to be distracted. The other driver may not be aware of your presence, and they may drift in front of you.

Texting While Driving

It is against the law to read, write, or send messages on a cell phone or other portable wireless device. If your cell phone rings, do not answer the call or respond to the text message. Convictions for violations of this law are subject to fines.

You may use a cell phone to contact law enforcement or during an emergency. If you must make a call, pull safely off the road and make the call. Try to keep the conversation short, or have a passenger make the call for you, if possible.

Chapter 10: Alcohol and Drug Impact on the Driving Ability

Any drug may affect a person's ability to drive. Millions of people take over the counter and prescription medications, illegal drugs, or drink alcohol and do not realize they may affect the mental and physical (psychomotor) skills necessary to operate a vehicle and react to external events while driving a vehicle.

Each individual is different. The driving skills of persons taking the same drug may be affected differently. A driver's body weight, emotional state, amount of drug taken, and when the drug was taken will influence the driver's ability to assess an emergency situation or judge speed and distance. Safe driving always requires an observant eye, a steady hand, and a clear head.

When a person drinks alcohol or uses drugs, one of the first effects is they lose their judgement and their sight is impaired, causing slower reactions to sounds and the inability to judge another vehicle's speed. A person's ability to reason can all but disappear. Good judgment may be as simple as saying no to a friend who wants to race their car. However, if a person has been drinking alcohol or they are under the influence of drugs, their judgment may turn into, "Sure, take my car."

Taking more than one drug at the same time is even more dangerous since drugs may have a different overall cumulative effect, especially when alcohol is involved. Besides escalating the overall effects of the other drugs, alcohol can also mask the effects of those drugs, increasing a person's risk of poor decision making and/or slowing responsive reactions to situations. You should always check with a doctor or pharmacist before taking more than one type of drug or mixing drugs, especially tranquilizers or sedatives.

Table 25: Alcohol and Other Types of Drugs

Type	Description
Marijuana	Research shows even typical social doses of marijuana can affect concentration, judgment, and sensory and perceptual skills needed for careful driving. People who are under marijuana influence have impaired sensory and perceptual abilities.
Stimulants	Heavy amphetamine use may keep drivers awake and active for long periods of time. It also makes them less coordinated, edgy, and more likely to be involved in a car crash. Research shows typical social amounts of cocaine can produce lapses in attention and concentration. While caffeine can help drowsy drivers stay alert, it can't make a drunk driver sober. Studies show ordinary amounts of caffeine don't improve a drunk driver's ability to operate a vehicle.
Tranquilizers / Sedative-Hypnotics	Tranquilizers/Sedative-hypnotic drugs, including barbiturates, are powerful depressants, which calm people down or help them sleep. Tired or over-sedated drivers are not good drivers.
Over-the-counter drugs	Many over-the-counter drugs cause drowsiness in some people, which can affect their driving. Read the labels and be careful with antihistamines, other cold preparations, or any medicine that relaxes or promotes sleep.
Any drug	Any drug might affect your ability as a driver. If you take more than one drug or if you mix drugs, especially tranquilizers or other sedative-hypnotics with alcohol, you could be asking for trouble on the road and off. If you have doubts about a drug or drug mix, check with a doctor or pharmacist.
Alcohol	Each year alcohol, a depressant drug affecting coordination, judgment, perception, and emotional state, is responsible for a significant number of highway deaths. Alcohol increases the depressant effects of tranquilizers and barbiturates. Mixing these drugs, on or off the road, can be hazardous.

The Number One Killer is Alcohol

Driving While Intoxicated (DWI) is a problem affecting all Texans. According to the Calendar Year 2018 *Texas Motor Vehicle Traffic Crash Facts* (TxDOT), 940 persons were killed in a motor vehicle traffic crash with a driver under the influence of alcohol. Alcohol related crashes represent 26% of the total number of persons killed in motor vehicle traffic crashes.

The Centers for Disease Control (CDC) states that the leading cause of death for U.S. teens is accidental and most of those are motor vehicle crashes. According to the National Highway Traffic Safety Administration (NHTSA), 3,255 teen (age 15 to 19) drivers were involved in fatal crashes in 2017 and nearly 25% of those had been drinking.

In 2018, TxDOT reports that nearly 7% of all fatal crashes involved a driver under the age of 21 who was under the influence of alcohol. Texas law does not allow any amount of blood alcohol concentration (BAC) for minors.

To make Texas safer, the Texas legislature enacted laws to deter people from drinking and driving by penalizing those who choose to drink and drive. In Texas, a person, age 21 and over, is considered legally intoxicated if the person has a BAC of 0.08 or more. Driving While Intoxicated (DWI) and Driving Under the Influence (DUI) arrests can be a humiliating experience and are costly. Some fines range as high as $10,000 not including the cost of a bail bondsman, attorney, or other court-required expenses. Is it worth the risk?

Open Container

It is illegal to possess an open container of alcohol in a motor vehicle passenger area located on a public highway, regardless of whether the vehicle is being operated, stopped, or parked. Conviction of this offense is punishable by a fine not to exceed $500.

Myths about Drinking Alcohol

Taking cold showers, drinking black coffee, or exercising will not make a person sober. Only time, based on body weight, number of drinks, and food intake can minimize the effects of alcohol. It takes about one hour for the body to rid itself of each drink consumed. If a person has been drinking, someone who has not been drinking should drive.

Texas Tough Alcohol-Related Laws for Minors

Zero Tolerance for Minors

According to the Texas Alcohol Beverage Code, a minor is any individual who is under 21 years of age. A minor may not purchase, attempt to purchase, consume, or possess an alcoholic beverage. Since a minor should not possess alcohol, Texas passed zero tolerance legislation for minors who commit an offense under the non-driving alcohol-related laws and for minors who drive under the influence.

Zero tolerance means just that. Even if a minor is not intoxicated as defined under the DWI statute, but has any detectable amount of alcohol in his/her system while operating a motor vehicle in a public place or while operating a water- craft, the minor committed the criminal offense of Driving Under the Influence of Alcohol by a Minor (see Table 31).

Penalties for Non-Driving Alcohol-Related Offenses by Minors

The Texas Zero Tolerance law established penalties for minors who commit offenses under the non-driving alcohol-related offenses. A minor may not purchase, attempt to purchase, falsely state he/she is 21 years of age or older, or present any document indicating he/she is 21 years of age or older to a person engaged in the selling or serving of alcoholic beverages. A minor may not consume, or possess an alcoholic beverage. Persons who purchase, furnish, or sell alcohol to a minor can be fined up to $4,000 and/or confined in jail for up to one year.

Table 26: Penalties for Non-Driving Alcohol-Related Offenses – Minors

Offense	Penalty
1st offense	Class C misdemeanor punishable by a fine of up to $500, 8 to 12 hours of community service, mandatory attendance of an alcohol awareness course, and license will be suspended (or privilege denied if not licensed) for 30 days. If the minor is under 18, the parent may be required to also attend the alcohol awareness course.
2nd offense	Class C misdemeanor punishable by a fine of up to $500, 20 to 40 hours of community service, may be required to attend an alcohol awareness course, and license will be suspended (or privilege denied if not licensed) for 60 days.
3rd offense (Under 17 years of age)	Class C misdemeanor punishable by a fine of up to $500, 20 to 40 hours of community service, may be required to attend an alcohol awareness course, and license will be suspended (or privilege denied if not licensed) for 60 days or case can be transferred to Juvenile Court.
3rd offense (17 to 21 years of age)	Class B misdemeanor punishable by a fine of $250 to $2,000, 40 to 60 hours of community service, may be required to attend an alcohol awareness course, confinement in jail not to exceed 180 days, and license will be suspended (or privilege denied if not licensed) for 180 days. Minors are not eligible for deferred disposition or adjudication on the third conviction and every conviction after.

In addition to the above penalties, if a minor is convicted of any moving vehicle violation while suspended due to a non-driving alcohol-related offense (listed above) they are subject to the penalties of Driving While License Invalid (DWLI).

Implied Consent Laws for Minors

A minor implies their consent to take one or more breath or blood specimen for analysis if they are arrested for operating a motor vehicle or watercraft in a public place while intoxicated, or if there is any detectable or noticeable amount of alcohol in their system while operating a motor vehicle in a public place as deemed by an officer. The breath or blood specimen will determine if alcohol is present in their body. It will also identify the amount of alcohol in their system. Additionally, the breath or blood specimen can identify the presence of any other controlled substances or drugs.

Refusal to provide a breath or blood specimen will result in the suspension of the minor's license or driving privileges if not licensed.

Table 27: Penalties for Refusal to Provide a Specimen - Minors

Offense	Penalty
1st offense	Driver license suspended (or privilege denied if not licensed) for 180 days.
2nd and subsequent offenses	Driver license suspended (or privilege denied if not licensed) for 2 years.

A minor who gives a breath or blood specimen that confirms he/she has been operating a motor vehicle in a public place with any detectable amount of alcohol in his/her system and the amount is below the 0.08 BAC legal limit of intoxication will have his/her license suspended or driving privilege denied if not licensed.

Table 28: Minor Provided Specimen Confirming Detectable Amount of Alcohol (failure)

Offense	Penalty
1st offense	Driver license suspended (or privilege denied if not licensed) for 60 days.
2nd offense	Driver license suspended (or privilege denied if not licensed) for 120 days.
3rd and subsequent offenses	Driver license suspended (or privilege denied if not licensed) for 180 days.

A minor may request a hearing before a hearing officer to contest the suspension.

Table 29: Penalties for Driving Under the Influence (DUI) of Alcohol and Drugs– Minors

Offense	Penalty
1st offense	Class C misdemeanor punishable by a fine of up to $500, community service of 20 to 40 hours, and attendance in an alcohol awareness course is required. If the minor is under 18, the parent may be required to also attend the course.
2nd offense	Class C misdemeanor punishable by a fine of up to $500, community service of 40 to 60 hours. The alcohol awareness course may be required.
3rd offense (under 17 years of age)	Class C misdemeanor punishable by a fine of up to $500, community service of 40 to 60 hours. The alcohol awareness course may be required or the case can be transferred to Juvenile Court as delinquent conduct.
3rd offense (17 to 21 years of age)	Class B misdemeanor punishable by a fine of $500 to $2,000 and/or confinement in jail not to exceed 180 days, community service of 40 to 60 hours, an alcohol awareness course may be required, and the minor's license will be suspended (or privilege denied of not licensed) for one year or for 90 days with a judge's order to install an ignition interlock device. The court may not give deferred disposition or adjudication on the third offense.

See Table 29 and Table 30 for the applicable suspension periods

In Texas, as a reminder, a person is considered legally intoxicated if they have a blood alcohol concentration (BAC) of 0.08 or more.

Table 30: Penalties for Driving While Intoxicated (Alcohol) – Minors

Offense	Penalty
1st offense	Class B misdemeanor punishable by a fine not to exceed $2,000, confinement in jail for 72 hours to 180 days, and suspension of the driver license (or privilege denied if not licensed) for 365 days, or for 90 days with a judge's order to install an ignition interlock device. The court may probate the jail sentence and waive the license suspension on the first offense only. Possession of an open container of an alcoholic beverage increases the minimum confinement to six days.
2nd offense	Class A misdemeanor punishable by a fine not to exceed $4,000, confinement in jail for 30 days to 1 year, and suspension of the driver license (or privilege denied if not licensed) for 180 days to 18 months.
3rd offense and every offense after	Felony of the third degree punishable by a fine not to exceed $10,000, imprisonment in the Texas Department of Criminal Justice (TDCJ) for 2 to 10 years, and suspension of the driver license (or privilege denied if not licensed) for 180 days to 18 months.
DWI with passenger under 15	A state jail felony punishable by a fine not to exceed $10,000, confinement in state jail for 180 days to 2 years and suspension of the driver license (or privilege denied if not licensed) for 90 days to 1 year.
Intoxication assault	Third degree felony punishable by a fine not to exceed $10,000, imprisonment in the Texas Department of Criminal Justice (TDCJ) for 2 to 10 years, and suspension of the driver license (or privilege denied if not licensed) for 90 days to 1 year.
Intoxication manslaughter	Second degree felony punishable by a fine not to exceed $10,000, imprisonment in the Texas Department of Criminal Justice (TDCJ) for 2 to 20 years, and a suspension of the driver license (or privilege denied if not licensed) for 180 days to 2 years.

Texas Alcohol-Related Laws for Adults

Implied Consent Laws for Adults

The implied consent for adults is similar to that of minors.

Like the minor, an adult implies their consent to take one or more breath or blood specimen for analysis if they are arrested for operating a motor vehicle or watercraft in a public place while intoxicated, or if they are an adult up to 21 years of age and there is any detectable or noticeable amount of alcohol in their system while operating a motor vehicle in a public place as deemed by an officer. The breath or blood specimen determines if alcohol is present in their body and will identify the amount of alcohol in their system, as well as the presence of any other controlled substances or drugs.

A person who refuses to give a blood or breath specimen for analysis will have their driver license suspended for 180 days or up to 730 days for subsequent offenses. If a person submits to a blood or breath specimen and the results show a BAC of 0.08 or greater, their driver license may be suspended for 90 days or up to 365 days for subsequent offenses. Anyone with a BAC of 0.08 or more is considered intoxicated.

Table 31: Penalties for DWI and DUI of Alcohol or Drugs-Adults

Offense	Fine	Confinement	Driver License Suspension
1st offense	Up to $2,000	72 hours to 180 days in jail	90 days to 365 days
2nd offense	Up to $4,000	30 days to 1 year in jail	180 days to 2 years
3rd and subsequent offenses	Up to $10,000	2 to 10 years in TDCJ	180 days to 2 years
DWI with passenger under 15	Up to $10,000	180 days to 2 years in state jail	90 days to 2 years
Intoxication assault	Up to $10,000	2 to 10 years in TDCJ	90 days to 2 years
Intoxication manslaughter	Up to $10,000	2 to 20 years in TDCJ	180 days to 2 years

Know Your Legal Limit

The legal limit in Texas is 0.08 BAC or any amount which results in the loss of normal use of mental or physical faculties. The information provided in the *Alcohol and Driving. Why Take the Risk?* table below is only a guide and is based on calculated averages. Alcohol tolerance may vary by individual. Food intake, medications, health, gender and psychological conditions are also influential factors, which affect the rate of alcohol absorption.

Drivers are encouraged to take drug and alcohol awareness courses to become better educated about the effects and consequences of drugs and alcohol. Insurance companies may provide liability insurance discounts to drivers who complete drug and alcohol awareness courses.

Table 32: Alcohol and Driving. Why Take the Risk?

Drinks	Body Weight in Pounds								Influenced
	100	120	140	160	180	200	220	240	
1	.04	.03	.03	.02	.02	.02	.02	.02	Possibly
2	.06	.06	.05	.05	.04	.04	.03	.03	Possibly
3	.11	.09	.08	.07	.06	.06	.05	.05	Impaired
4	.15	.12	.11	.09	.08	.08	.07	.06	Impaired
5	.19	.16	.13	.12	.11	.09	.09	.08	Legally intoxicated
6	.23	.19	.16	.14	.13	.11	.10	.09	Legally intoxicated
7	.26	.22	.19	.16	.15	.13	.12	.11	Legally intoxicated
8	.30	.25	.21	.19	.17	.15	.14	.13	Legally intoxicated
9	.34	.28	.24	.21	.19	.17	.15	.14	Legally intoxicated
10	.38	.31	.27	.23	.21	.19	.17	.16	Legally intoxicated

A drink may include a 12 ounce can of beer, a mixed drink with 1.5 ounces of liquor or a 5 ounce glass of wine. They all contain approximately the same amount of alcohol.

Chapter 11: Motor Vehicle Crashes

Most crashes in Texas result from speeding, failure to yield or stop appropriately, and driving under the influence of alcohol. If requested and available, exchange names, addresses, phone numbers, vehicle identification numbers, vehicle license plate numbers, driver license information, and insurance information with all drivers involved in the crash. Write the insurance company name and policy number exactly as it is shown on the driver's proof-of-insurance card. If you have the name of the driver's insurance company and the information is not listed directly on the insurance card, call the Texas Department of Insurance at (800) 252-3439 to get the company address and telephone number. Be sure to also note the location of the crash and write down the contact information if there are any witnesses.

You should always notify the appropriate law enforcement agency as soon as possible when:

- There is an injury or fatality
- The vehicles involved cannot be moved off the roadway
- A driver leaves the scene of the crash
- You suspect a driver is intoxicated.

If you are involved in a crash that is not investigated by a law enforcement officer and the crash has not resulted in injury or death of a person or damage to property of $1,000 or more, you must make a written report of the crash and file it with the Texas Department of Transportation (TxDOT) no later than the 10th day after the date of the crash. The written report must be on a TxDOT specified form. For a copy of this form, please visit the TxDOT website at www.txdot.gov.

Crash Resulting in Injury to, or Death of a person

If you are operating a motor vehicle involved in a crash resulting in injury to or death of a person, you must immediately stop your vehicle at the scene of the crash (or as close as possible to the scene of the crash) without obstructing traffic more than necessary. If you did not stop your vehicle at the scene, you must immediately return and remain at the scene of the crash until you have complied with the following:

1. Provide your name and address, the registration number of the vehicle you were driving, and the name of your motor vehicle liability insurer to any person injured, or to the operator or occupant of, or person attending a vehicle involved in the collision

2. Show your driver license (if requested and available) to any person injured, or to the operator or occupant of, or person attending a vehicle involved in the collision

3. Provide any person injured in the crash reasonable assistance including, transporting or making arrangements for transporting the person to a physician or hospital for medical treatment, if it is apparent treatment is necessary, or if the injured person requests the transportation.

Table 33: Penalties for Failure to Stop

Offense	Penalty
1st offense crash resulting in a death of a person	Second degree felony punishable by a fine not to exceed $10,000 and imprisonment in the Texas Department of Criminal Justice (TDCJ) for 2 to 20 years.
1st offense crash resulting in serious bodily injury	Third degree felony punishable by a fine not to exceed $10,000 and imprisonment in the Texas Department of Criminal Justice (TDCJ) for 2 to 10 years.
1st offense crash resulting in injury	Imprisonment in the Texas Department of Criminal Justice (TDCJ) for up to 5 years or confinement in the county jail for up to 1 year; a fine not to exceed $5,000; or both a fine and imprisonment.

Crash Resulting in Damage to a Vehicle

If you are operating a motor vehicle involved in a crash resulting **ONLY** in damage to a vehicle that is driven or attended by a person, you must immediately stop your vehicle at the scene of the crash or as close as possible to the scene of the crash without obstructing traffic more than necessary. If the crash occurs on a main lane, ramp, shoulder, median, or adjacent area and each vehicle involved can be normally and safely driven, drivers must move their vehicle as soon as possible to a designated crash investigation site, if available, a location on the frontage road, the nearest suitable cross street, or other suitable location. If you did not stop your vehicle at the scene, you must immediately return and remain at the scene of the crash until you have complied with the following:

1. Provide your name and address, the registration number of the vehicle you were driving, and the name of your motor vehicle liability insurer to any person injured, or to the operator or occupant of, or person attending a vehicle involved in the collision

2. Show your driver license (if requested and available) to any operator or occupant of, or person attending a vehicle involved in the collision

Table 34: Penalties for Failure to Stop

Offense	Penalty
1st offense (Less than $200 in damages)	Class C misdemeanor and is punishable by a fine not to exceed $500.
1st offense ($200 or more in damages)	Class B misdemeanor and is punishable by a fine not to exceed $2,000, confinement in jail for up to 180 days, or both.

Crash Involving an Unattended Vehicle

If you are operating a motor vehicle that collides with and damages an unattended vehicle, you must immediately stop and either:

1. Locate the operator or owner of the unattended vehicle and give your name and address

2. Securely attach a written notice in a visible way to the unattended vehicle providing:

   • Your name and address

   • A statement of the circumstances of the collision.

Table 35: Penalties for Failure to Stop

Offense	Penalty
1st offense (Less than $200 in damages)	Class C misdemeanor and is punishable by a fine not to exceed $500.
1st offense ($200 or more in damages)	Class B misdemeanor and is punishable by a fine not to exceed $2,000, confinement in jail for up to 180 days, or both.

Crash Resulting in Damages to a Fixture, Landscaping, or Structure

If you are driving a motor vehicle involved in a crash resulting ONLY in damage to a fixture, landscaping, or structure legally on or adjacent to a highway, you must:

1. Take reasonable steps to locate the owner (or person in charge) of the property and notify him/her of the crash

2. Provide your name, address, and registration number of the vehicle you were driving

3. If requested and available, you must show your driver license to the owner or person in charge of the property

4. If the crash is not investigated by a law enforcement officer and the crash has not resulted in injury to or the death of a person or damage to the property of any one person to an apparent extent of $1,000 or more, you must make a written report of the crash and file it with the TxDOT no later than the 10th day after the crash.

Table 36: Penalties for Failure to Comply with Damages

Offense	Penalty
1st offense (Less than $200 in damages)	Class C misdemeanor and is punishable by a fine not to exceed $500.
1st offense ($200 or more in damages)	Class B misdemeanor and is punishable by a fine not to exceed $2,000, confinement in jail for up to 180 days, or both.

Hit-and-Run Crashes

If you are involved in a hit-and-run crash, report this crash to law enforcement for investigation. The Texas Department of Insurance advises uninsured motorist coverage will pay for damages in hit-and-run crashes reported to a law enforcement agency.

Aiding the Injured

In the event you are involved in a crash that injures another person, consider the information below:

1. When calling a doctor or ambulance, ensure you take notice of your surroundings and state the location of the crash clearly and correctly.

2. Do not assume people are not injured simply because they say they are not. Send for skilled help as quickly as possible. Un-skilled handling can do more harm than good.

3. Do not move or lift the victim(s) unless it is absolutely necessary. If a victim must be moved, get help and try not to change the position in which the victim was found.

4. Stop serious bleeding with thick cloth pads, as clean as possible, apply with pressure by hand or by bandaging.

5. Keep the victim(s) comfortable. If it is hot, cool the victim(s) and provide shade as much as possible. If it is cool, cover the victim with blankets or coats if necessary and if available.

Chapter 12: Pedestrian Safety

A driver should always pay special attention to pedestrians (persons on foot). However, there are certain safety rules pedestrians should follow.

Laws and Safety Tips for Pedestrians

1. Obey traffic control signals unless otherwise directed by a pedestrian control signal.

2. Do not cross the street between two intersections. It is dangerous to cross in the middle of a street.

3. Use sidewalks when available, and do not walk in the street.

4. Walk on the left side of the road if there are no sidewalks. Step off the pavement when a car approaches.

5. If you cross a street at any point other than within a crosswalk at an intersection, you (the pedestrian) must yield the right-of-way to all vehicles.

6. If you cross a street without using a pedestrian tunnel or overhead pedestrian crossing which has been provided, you (the pedestrian) must yield the right-of-way to all vehicles.

7. When crossing at a crosswalk, keep right if possible.

8. Blind, partially blind, or disabled individuals may carry a white cane while walking. Others must not display a white cane on any public street or highway.

9. No person may stand in the road for the purpose of soliciting a ride, contributions, or business. A person may stand in a road to solicit a charitable contribution if authorized to do so by the local authority having jurisdiction over the road.

10. Do not suddenly walk or run into the street in the path of a vehicle. These sudden actions may make it impossible for the vehicle operator to yield.

11. Wait on the curb, not in the street, until the traffic signals change to green or read "Walk."

12. Always wear white or light colored clothing and/or carry a light or reflector when walking at night.

13. Look both ways before crossing the street and before stepping out from behind parked cars.

14. Be extra careful when getting off a streetcar or bus.

15. Get in and out of cars on the curb side of the road when possible.

16. Do not walk on a road when you are under the influence or consuming an alcoholic beverage. Alcohol is a contributing factor to pedestrian traffic crashes.

17. Pedestrians should be aware that local authorities may have ordinances that require pedestrians to comply with the directions of an official traffic control device (signals, signs, etc.) and prohibit pedestrians from crossing a road in a business district or a designated highway, except in a crosswalk.

Laws and Safety Tips for Motorists

1. If you see a pedestrian crossing or attempting to cross the street, slow down, use your horn if necessary, and be prepared to stop.

2. Be alert to a pedestrian guided by an assistance animal or carrying a white cane. The white cane indicates the person may be blind, partially blind, or disabled. A driver shall take the necessary pre-cautions to avoid injuring or endangering a pedestrian crossing or attempting to cross the street. The driver shall bring the vehicle to a full stop if injury or danger can only be avoided by that action.

3. Watch for individuals who are blind at bus stops, intersections, business areas, and near schools for the blind.

Chapter 13: Bicycle Laws and Safety

Bicycle Traffic Laws

A bicycle is a vehicle. Any person riding a bicycle has the same rights and responsibilities that apply to a driver operating a vehicle unless these cannot, by their nature, apply to a person operating a bicycle.

Any person who operates a bicycle is subject to the same penalties for violating a traffic law as a person operating a motor vehicle. All traffic convictions will be placed on the individual's driver record, regardless if the conviction was for an offense committed on a bicycle or in a motor vehicle.

Do's

1. Always obey all traffic laws, signs, and signals. Stop at all stop signs and red lights.

2. Always ride with the flow of traffic.

3. Only ride on or astride a permanent and regular seat.

4. When operating a bicycle on a one-way road with two or more marked traffic lanes, ride as near as possible to the left curb or edge of the road.

5. Individuals riding two abreast on a "laned" road must ride in a single lane and not impede the flow of traffic.

6. Bicyclists may ride on the shoulder of the road.

7. Bicyclists must signal a turn or stop by:

   a. Using either their left arm pointing up or their right arm pointed horizontally to signal a right turn.

   b. Using their left arm pointed horizontally to signal a left turn.

   c. Using their left arm pointed downward to signal a stop.

8. A person operating a bicycle who is moving slower than the other traffic on the road shall ride as near as possible to the right curb or edge of the road unless:

   a. The person is overtaking and passing another vehicle proceeding in the same direction

   b. The person is preparing for a left turn at an intersection or onto a private road or driveway

   c. There are unsafe conditions in the road such as fixed or moving objects, parked or moving vehicles, pedestrians, animals, potholes, or debris, or

   d. The person is operating a bicycle in an outside lane that is:

      - Less than 14 feet in width and doesn't have a designated bicycle lane adjacent to that lane; or

      - The lane is too narrow for a bicycle and a motor vehicle to safely travel side by side.

Don'ts

1. Never carry more than the number of individuals it is designated or equipped for.

2. Never ride opposite the flow of traffic.

3. Never attach the bicycle or person to a moving streetcar or vehicle upon a road.

4. Never carry any package, bundle, or article which prevents the rider from keeping at least one hand on the handlebars.

Shared Lane Marking

Shared Lane Marking

The shared lane marking may be used to:

1. Assist bicyclists with lateral positioning in a shared lane with on-street parallel parking in order to reduce the chance of a bicyclist impacting the open door of a parked vehicle

2. Assist bicyclists with lateral position in lanes too narrow for a motor vehicle and a bicycle to travel side by side within the same traffic lane

3. Alert road users of the lateral location bicyclists are likely to occupy within the traveled way

4. Encourage safe passing of bicyclists by motorists, or

5. Reduce the incidence of wrong-way bicycling

Bicycles Must Be Properly Equipped

1. Every bicycle must be equipped with a brake, which will enable the operator to make the wheels skid on dry, level, clean pavement when applied.

2. Hearing-impaired bicycle riders may display a safety flag.

3. Every bicycle used at nighttime must be equipped with:

    a. A lamp on the front emits a white light visible from a distance of at least 500 feet in front of the bicycle, and

    b. A red, DPS-approved reflector on the rear visible from distances of 50 feet to 300 feet. (A red light on the rear visible from a distance of 500 feet may be used in addition to the red reflector.)

Bicycle Safety Guidelines

1. You may be required by law to wear a helmet depending on your local laws.

2. When riding on pedestrian facilities, reduce speed and exercise caution.

3. Do not weave in and out of parked cars.

4. Move off the street to stop, park, or make repairs to your bicycle.

5. Select a route according to the rider's bicycling skill and experience.

6. Bicycles may be equipped with a mirror.

7. Wear light colored or reflective clothing to make it easier for drivers to see you.

Riding in Wet Weather

Water makes certain surfaces slick. Be aware of manhole covers and painted stripes on the road. Water also obscures some hazards. Watch for potholes filled with water. In addition, the visibility of motorists is greatly decreased in wet weather.

Chapter 14: Additional Safety Tips

Defensive Driving

To avoid crashes, the defensive driver should:

1. Stay alert and keep eyes moving to keep track of what is happening at all times

2. Look for trouble spots developing all around

3. Have a plan of action

4. Know that the law requires drivers to protect each other from their own mistakes

Safety Belts

The driver and all passengers, regardless of age, in a passenger vehicle are required to use safety belts if occupying a seat in a vehicle equipped with a safety belt. Any child under 8 years old must be secured in a federally approved child car seat if occupying a seat in a vehicle equipped with a safety belt, unless the child is more than 4'9" tall.

Safety belt requirements include pickups, SUVs, and trucks. Safety belts help keep you:

1. From being thrown from your car. Your chances of being killed are five times greater if you are thrown from your car

2. From hitting the dashboard too hard

3. In better control of your car

Whatever your reason for not wearing safety belts, it is dangerous and violates state law.

**FASTEN
SAFETY
BELTS
STATE LAW**

Penalties for Driving Without a Safety Belt

A driver can receive a citation for not wearing his/her safety belt and for not having each child under the age of 17 in a safety seat or safety belt. Anyone who is at least 15 years of age can receive a citation for not wearing a safety belt. There are no exemptions to the safety belt laws. However, there are some defenses to prosecution for postal workers, individuals who deliver the newspaper, utility workers, solid waste truck workers, certain commercial farm vehicle operators, or medical reasons with a physician's note.

Table 37: Penalties for Not Wearing a Required Safety Belt

Conviction	Penalty*
Driving a vehicle without a safety belt	A fine of $25 to $50
Passengers under 8 years old and less than 4'9" tall riding while not properly secured in a child passenger safety seat system	A fine of $25 to $250
Passengers at least 15 years old riding without a safety belt	A fine of $25 to $50
Passengers under 17 years old riding without a safety belt (fine assessed to driver)	A fine of $100 to $200
Children under 18 years old riding in an open-bed pickup or open flatbed truck (fine assessed to driver)	A fine of $25 to $200

*Additional suspensions may apply.

Vehicles with Open Beds

It is an offense to drive an open bed truck, an open flatbed truck, or to draw an open flatbed trailer when a child who is younger than 18 years of age is occupying the bed of the truck or trailer.

It is a defense to prosecution that the driver was operating or towing the vehicle:

1. In a parade or in an emergency

2. To transport farm-workers from one field to another field on a farm-to-market road, ranch-to-market road, or county road outside a municipality

3. On a beach

4. That is the only vehicle owned or operated by members of a household, or

5. In a hayride permitted by the governing body of or a law enforcement agency of each county or municipality in which the hayride will occur

Vehicles with Open Beds Towing a Boat or Watercraft

It is an offense for a person to operate a motor vehicle that is towing a boat or personal watercraft in or on which a person who is younger than 18 years of age is riding.

It is a defense to prosecution that the driver was operating the motor vehicle:

1. In a parade

2. In an emergency, or

3. On a beach

Open Bed Passenger Restrictions

It is a Class B misdemeanor to operate a truck, road tractor, or truck tractor when another person occupies a trailer or semi-trailer being drawn by the truck, road tractor, or truck tractor.

It is a defense to prosecution that the person:

1. Towing the vehicle did not know another person occupied the trailer or semi-trailer

2. Occupying the trailer or semi-trailer was in a part of the vehicle designed for human habitation

3. Operating or towing the vehicle was:

   a. In a parade or in an emergency

   b. Transporting farm-workers from one field to another field on a farm-to-market road, ranch-to-market road, or county road outside a municipality, or

   c. In a hayride permitted by the governing body of or a law enforcement agency of each county or municipality in which the hayride will occur

When Stopped by Law Enforcement

If you are stopped by law enforcement, it is suggested you:

1. Slow down and move the vehicle safely to the right of the road.

2. Park your vehicle as far to the right of the main traffic lane as possible. If available, park on the right shoulder or, if unavailable, park on a nearby well-lighted side street or parking lot away from high volume traffic.

3. Place the vehicle in a parking position, set the emergency brake, turn the engine off, and activate the hazard warning lights.

4. If at night, turn on the interior dome light.

5. Remain in the car, lower the driver's window if you feel safe to do so. Keep both hands clearly in sight on top of the steering wheel. Wait for the law enforcement officer to give you instructions. An officer may approach from either side of the vehicle.

6. Tell the officer if you are transporting any type of weapon.

7. Before reaching into your glove box or under the seat to retrieve your proof of insurance or driver's license, inform the officer of where the items are located and follow the officer's directions.

8. If asked to exit the vehicle, check for passing vehicles to exit safely.

9. Advise passengers to remain in the car unless other instructions are given by the law enforcement officer, and

10. At the conclusion of the traffic stop, give the appropriate signals and safely return to the proper lane of traffic when released by the law enforcement officer.

Obligations, Responsibilities, Courtesy and Safety

State law requires a driver to immediately stop when approached by an authorized emergency vehicle and you may be arrested if you do not stop immediately. If you feel the area is unsafe to stop immediately or if you have concerns the vehicle is not a real police vehicle, you can take the following steps to minimize the risk of being arrested or charges being filed against you: turn on your hazard lights and drive slowly and carefully below the posted speed limit; you may call 9-1-1 and remain on the phone with the operator while you stop and verify the officer's identity; you may drive to a nearby well-lighted, populated place to stop. It is important to understand that law enforcement jurisdictions overlap and a local 9-1-1 call center operator may not be able to immediately determine what officer is working in that area at that time. If you stop in an unsafe location, such as on a bridge or a high traffic roadway, an officer may direct you over the public address speaker to move to a safer location. Follow the officer's directions.

Law enforcement officers, drivers, and passengers should respond with courtesy during traffic stops and other officer/citizen interactions. Drivers and passengers should not exit the vehicle unless asked to do so. Exiting your vehicle may be perceived as aggressive behavior and a threat to the officer's safety. Drivers and passengers inside a vehicle should not attempt to reach, dig, or search for their license or insurance documents before or while an officer is approaching. Drivers who transport handguns in their vehicles are encouraged to keep them in a separate location from license and insurance documentation.

During a traffic stop, the driver and any passengers are subjected to an investigative detention, which may only last for a reasonable amount of time. Passengers can ask the officer if they are free to leave and do so if the officer agrees. Law enforcement may ask questions during this time. You cannot be punished for refusing to answer questions; however, drivers are required by law to display a driver license when requested by an officer. If you are lawfully arrested, you are also required to give your name, residence address, and date of birth. A driver or a passenger who gives law enforcement a false or fraudulent identity or false answers may be arrested. It may be to your benefit to speak to law enforcement, such as to convey the reason you may have an emergency or for the driver to provide the officer your name, address and date of birth if you do not have your driver license with you.

Law enforcement may also ask for consent to search your vehicle or person. You may grant or deny the request to search; however, if an officer has probable cause to believe that your vehicle contains evidence of a crime, it can be searched without your consent. If an officer reasonably believes that you have a weapon, the officer can conduct a pat down search of your person and the immediate area around you, including areas of your vehicle. It is unlawful to physically resist a search, but you have the right to notify the officer that you do not consent to any search.

Complaints or Concerns

If you believe an officer has acted inappropriately during a traffic stop or other encounter, you should report that conduct to the officer's superiors and follow agency guidelines for submitting complaints against officers as soon as possible. Officers will normally provide their names and badge numbers on request, when practical. Due to the overlapping of jurisdictions, drivers should make sure they identify the correct agency as well as any identifying aspects of the officer and law enforcement vehicle.

Drivers should refrain from arguing the validity of a charge during the traffic stop or detention. Signing a citation is not admitting guilt. It simply confirms your promise to pay the fine or contact the court. If you do not agree with the charge brought against you and wish to contest it, you should argue your case before a judge or request a jury trial and acquire the services of an attorney to represent you.

False Identification Offense

A person commits an offense if he/she gives a false or fictitious name to a law enforcement officer who has lawfully arrested or detained the person.

Evading arrest or detention

A person commits an offense if he intentionally flees from a person he knows is a peace officer or federal special investigator attempting to lawfully arrest or detain him/her. You will be subject to higher penalties if you use a vehicle or watercraft while evading arrest or cause injury to another person.

Road Rage

Each year, road rage, also referred to as aggressive driving, causes hundreds of injuries and deaths. Aggressive driving occurs when a driver becomes angry or irritated and as a result, fails to follow the rules of the road. An aggressive driver will intentionally aggravate or attempt to aggravate other drivers and in some cases cause bodily injury, property damage, or death to others.

Tips to Avoid Road Rage

1. Plan your trip or schedule in advance. Allow extra time in case your vehicle breaks down or you encounter traffic congestion due to a crash, road construction, or rush-hour traffic.

2. When caught in traffic, do not get angry. Try to relax and listen to music you enjoy. Remember, traffic congestion is usually temporary and you will soon be on your way.

3. Should you need to use the horn, tap the horn; do not hold down the horn. Do not confront other drivers or make obscene gestures.

4. Do not cut into another driver's lane of traffic. Properly signal your intentions to change lanes and change lanes when it is safe to do so. Turn your turn signal off after you complete your lane change.

5. Do not intentionally slow down, slam on your brakes, or speed up to keep someone from passing or entering your lane of travel.

6. Do not tailgate; follow at a safe distance.

7. Always remember to drive friendly and report aggressive driving to the local authorities.

Neighborhood Electronic Vehicles and Motor Assisted Scooters

A neighborhood electronic vehicle is defined as a vehicle subject to Federal Motor Safety Standard 500 with a top speed of 35 mph on a paved level surface.

A motor assisted scooter is defined as a self-propelled device with:

1. At least two wheels in contact with the ground

2. A braking system capable of stopping the device under normal operating conditions

3. A gas or electric motor not exceeding 40 cc

4. A deck designed to allow a person to stand or sit while operating the device, and

5. The ability to be propelled by human power alone

Both vehicles may only be operated on a street or highway when the posted speed limit is 45 mph or less for a neighborhood electronic vehicle and 35 mph or less for a motor assisted scooter.

Electronic Personal Assistive Mobility Devices (EPAMD)

EPAMD's, such as a Segway, is defined as a two, non-tandem wheeled device designed for transporting one person that is self-balancing and propelled by an electric propulsion system with an average power of 750 watts or one horsepower.

Special Note: Counties and municipalities may prohibit the operation of either type of vehicle on any street or highway for safety reasons.

An EPAMD may be operated on:

1. A sidewalk

2. A path set aside for the exclusive operation of a bicycle

3. On a residential street, road, or public highway with a maximum speed limit of 30 mph only:

    a. While making a direct crossing of a highway in a marked or unmarked crosswalk

    b. Where no sidewalk is available, or

    c. When so directed by a traffic control device or law enforcement officer

When operated on a public roadway, an EPAMD shall be ridden as close as practicable to the right-hand edge.

Your Keys to Safe Driving

• Good Vision

• Obey traffic laws

• Proper care of vehicle – Don't depend on yearly inspections; perform regular maintenance as needed

• Courtesy – Safety comes before the right-of-way

• Proper Signaling – Failure to signal is dangerous and inconsiderate

• Fitness to drive – Let someone else drive if you are not physically or mentally alert

Transporting Cargo and Materials

To prevent cargo or loose materials from falling or spilling from a car, truck, trailer, etc. onto the road and causing a crash or damage to the roads, drivers must comply with certain state requirements.

A vehicle must be equipped and maintained to prevent loose material from escaping by blowing or spilling and a vehicle bed must:

1. Not have a hole, crack, or other opening through which loose material can escape

2. Be enclosed by side panels and on the front by a panel or the vehicle cab

3. Be enclosed by a securely closed tailgate or panel on the rear to prevent spillage

4. Cover the load securely at the front and back of the load, unless completely enclosed in a compartment or the load does not blow or spill over the load carrying compartment.

No person shall load or transport any loose material on or over the public highways, such as dirt, sand, gravel, wood chips, or other material (except agricultural products in their natural state), capable of blowing or spilling from a vehicle unless:

1. The bed carrying the load is completely enclosed on both sides and on the front and rear by a tailgate, board or panel; and all must be so constructed as to prevent the escape of any part of the load by blowing or spilling; and

2. The top of the load is covered with a canvas, tarpaulin, or other covering firmly secured to the front and back to prevent the escape of the load because of blowing or spilling. This requirement does not apply to:

    a. Any load-carrying compartment that completely encloses the load; or

    b. The transporting of any load of loose materials not blowing or spilling over the top of the load-carrying compartment.

Safety Chains

Safety chains are required when certain types of vehicles are towing trailers in order to prevent the trailer from breaking loose and causing a serious crash. A person may not drive a passenger car or light truck while towing a trailer, semi-trailer, or house trailer on a public highway in Texas unless safety chains are attached from a trailer, semi-trailer, or house trailer to the towing vehicle. The types of safety chains and the manner of attachment must be approved by DPS. The requirements of this law do not apply to a passenger car or light truck towing a trailer or semi-trailer used for agricultural purposes or to any trailer or semi-trailer or house trailer operated in compliance with the Federal Motor Carrier Safety Regulations.

Towing

When one vehicle is towing another, the drawbar, chain, rope, cable, or other connection must:

1. Not be longer than 15 feet from one vehicle to another

2. Be strong enough to pull all weight drawn

3. Attach a white flag not less than 12 inches square

4. Not tow more than three vehicles attached to it by mounting the front wheels of trailing vehicles on the bed of another vehicle and leaving only the rear wheels in contact with the roadway

This limit does not apply to trailers transporting poles, pipes, machinery, or other structures that cannot be easily dismembered.

Carbon Monoxide

Beware of carbon monoxide poisoning. Cars produce carbon monoxide, which is a deadly gas. Make sure you are getting plenty of fresh air.

Don't:

1. Leave the motor running in a garage

2. Leave vents open when following closely behind another car

3. Leave the motor running and the windows closed while the car is parked

4. Drive with a defective muffler or exhaust system

5. Use the heater or air conditioner in a parked car with the windows closed in an enclosed space

If you encounter a carbon monoxide poisoning victim, move them to fresh air and call 911.

As a driver, you should know all the safety and operational features of the vehicle you are driving. Make sure you and your passengers are traveling in a vehicle that is safe and in good working order. Drive safely and obey all criminal and traffic laws.

Driving with Disability Program

Communication Impediment with a Peace Officer is an optional restriction code offered on Texas State ID and Driver License for those wanting to alert law enforcement of a challenge with communication. Physician signed form required.

If you want to place the code for "Communication Impediment with a Peace Officer" on your Texas ID or driver license, ask your doctor to complete form DL-101 https://www.dps.texas.gov/internetforms/Forms/DL-101.pdf and present it at the driver license office. The code will go on the back of your license, similar to other codes like organ donor or corrective lenses.

The option for disclosure of a communication disability/impediment when registering a vehicle through the Texas Department of Motor Vehicles is also available, the communication impediment will then be privately placed in the Texas Law Enforcement Telecommunication System (TLETS) thus alerting the officer of the challenge PRIOR to approaching the vehicle in a pull-over scenario. Form VTR-216 https://www.txdmv.gov/sites/default/files/form_files/VTR-216.pdf must be completed by a licensed physician if the applicant has a physical health condition or a licensed physician, licensed psychologist, or a non-physician mental health professional if the applicant has a mental health condition. Present this form when you register your vehicle with Texas DMV.

For more information on Driving with Disability Program please visit: Texas Driving with Disability | Office of the Texas Governor | Greg Abbott https://gov.texas.gov/organization/disabilities/texas-driving-with-disability

Appendix A: Glossary of Terms

- A -

acceleration lane – a lane that permits drivers entering a highway to accelerate to the speed of traffic

aggressive driving – the behavior of driving in a combative, forceful, or competitive manner

angle parking – the vehicle is parked diagonally to the curb

auto cycle – an autocycle constitutes a motor vehicle, other than a tractor, that is:
1. designed to have when propelled not more than three wheels on the ground
2. equipped with a steering wheel
3. equipped with seating that does not require the operator to straddle or sit astride the seat; and
4. manufactured and certified to comply with federal safety requirements for a motorcycle

An autocycle can be operated under a Class C driver license

- B -

backup lights – white lights at the rear of the vehicle telling other drivers you are backing up

basic speed law – you may not drive faster than is safe and prudent for existing conditions, regardless of posted speed limits

bicycle – every device propelled by human power upon which any person may ride, having two tandem wheels either of which is more than 14 inches in diameter

blind spot – an area rearview mirrors cannot show

blood-alcohol concentration (BAC) – the amount of alcohol in the blood expressed as a percentage of ethyl alcohol related to the volume of fluids in the bloodstream

blowout – the sudden loss of tire air pressure while driving

bodily-injury insurance – covers the driver who is at fault against claims

braking distance – the distance a vehicle travels from the time brakes are applied until it stops

- C -

cancellation – the withdrawal of a driver license or privilege until the driver is qualified or eligible

carbon monoxide – colorless, odorless, tasteless gas contained in the exhaust fumes of gasoline engines

center of gravity – point around which the vehicle's weight is evenly distributed

central vision – the field of vision around your focal vision in which you can see clearly while looking straight ahead that aids in determining vehicle position to the road

clutch pedal – the pedal in a manual transmission vehicle that enables a driver to shift gears

collision – contact between two or more objects, as when two vehicles collide into each other

collision insurance – provides insurance coverage to pay the costs of repair or replacement of your vehicle involved in a collision

color-blindness – inability to distinguish colors

commercial motor vehicle – a vehicle used to transport/deliver goods or passengers for compensation between points on a fixed scheduled route. The vehicle:
1. has a gross combination weight or gross combination weight rating of 26,001 or more pounds, including a towed unit with a gross vehicle weight or gross vehicle weight rating of more than 10,000 pounds;
2. has a gross vehicle weight or a gross vehicle weight rating of 26,001 or more pounds;
3. is designed to transport 16 or more passengers, including the driver or
4. is transporting hazardous materials and is required to be placarded under 49 C.F.R. part 172, Subpart F.

comprehensive insurance – provides coverage for replacement or repair of your vehicle from damage other than from a collision

controlled-access highway – a highway where vehicles can enter and exit only at interchanges

controlled braking – reducing speed by firmly stepping on and squeezing the brake pedal and maintaining steering control of the vehicle

controlled intersection – the intersection at which signals or signs determine the right of way

controlled railroad crossing – railroad crossing controlled by flashing red lights and/or crossing gates

crossbuck – large white X-shaped sign located prior to a railroad crossing

- D -

deceleration lane – expressway lane used to slow your vehicle without blocking vehicles behind you

defensive driving – protecting yourself and others from dangerous and unexpected driving situations by using a space management system

delayed green light – indicates one side of the intersection has a green light while the light for oncoming traffic remains red

denial – the withholding of a driver license or privilege because the person is ineligible for a license. A driver license may be issued when eligibility requirements are met.

depressant – a drug or alcohol that slows the response of the central nervous system

depth perception – the ability to judge distance between yourself and other objects

designated driver – the person who decides ahead of time not to drink alcoholic beverages and is appointed to drive others who do drink

distractions – when a driver is delayed in the recognition of information needed to accomplish the driving task safely because some event, activity, object, or person within or outside the vehicle compelled or tended to induce the driver's shifting attention away from the driving task

drag race – the operation of:
   1. Two or more vehicles from a point side by side at accelerating speeds in a competitive attempt to outdistance each other; or
   2. One or more vehicles over a common selected course, from the same place to the same place, for the purpose of comparing speeds or power of acceleration of the vehicle(s) in a specified distance of time

driving under the influence (DUI) – a Class C misdemeanor for which a minor can be charged in Texas if driving with any detectable amount of alcohol in the minor's system (An offense for which a driver can be charged in some states if the driver's blood-alcohol concentration is above 0.05.)

driving while intoxicated (DWI) – an offense for which a driver can be charged in all states if the driver's blood-alcohol concentration is above a certain level

- E -

entrance ramp – a ramp leading onto a highway

exit ramp – a ramp leading off a highway

- F -

field of vision – all the area a person can see while looking straight ahead.

field sobriety test – series of on-the-spot, road-side tests that help an officer detect impairment of a driver suspected of DUI or DWI.

financial responsibility law – a law requiring you to prove you can pay for collision damages you cause that result in death, injury, or property damage

flashing signal – traffic signal alerting drivers to dangerous conditions or tells them to stop

focus vision (fovial) – the part of the vision field which allows the driver to read signs and make distinctions between vehicles and objects often measured as visual acuity

following interval – the time recommended to follow another vehicle in the intended path of travel. Select an object near the road surface. When the vehicle ahead passes that object, start counting one thousand-one, one thousand-two, etc., until the front of your car reaches the same object. For speeds under 30 mph, the minimum time with good road conditions is 2 seconds. For speeds above 30 mph, maintain 4 seconds (more for adverse conditions) of following time. Developing a four-second following interval is the best practice for a beginning or less experienced driver

force of impact – the force with which one moving object hits another object; this varies according to speed, weight, and distance between impact and stop, and is based on forces of inertia and momentum

friction – the force creating heat which helps the tire maintain traction on the road, unless too much heat is generated which may cause traction loss due to melting of tire rubber on the road

- G -

gap – time or distance interval between vehicles on road

glare recovery time – the time your eyes need to regain clear vision after being affected by bright lights

glare resistance – the ability to continue seeing when looking at bright lights

graduated driver license program – requires young drivers to progress through a series of licensing stages with various restrictions such as accompanying drivers, times permitted to drive, and allowable passengers

guide sign – a sign providing directions, distances, services, points of interest, or other information

- H -

hallucinogen – mind-altering drug that tends to distort a person's perception of direction, distance, and time

hazard flasher – a device that flashes front turn signal lights and taillights to warn others the vehicle is a hazard

head restraints – specially designed air bag or padded devices on the backs of front seats helping to reduce whiplash injuries in a side or rear impact collision

highway hypnosis – drowsy or trance-like condition caused by concentration on the road ahead and monotony of driving

hydroplaning – occurs when a tire patch loses contact with the road by rising up on top of water

highway – the width between the boundary lines of a publicly maintained way any part of which is open to the public for vehicular travel

- I -

ignition interlock device – a special mechanical control device installed on a motor vehicle's dashboard. A driver must exhale into the device to start the vehicle. The court-ordered installation of an interlock ignition device must be performed by a DPS-certified service center

implied-consent law – anyone who receives a driver license automatically consents to be tested for blood-alcohol content and other drugs if stopped for suspicion of alcohol or drug usage while driving

intoxilyzer – the breath-test instrument machine commonly used for determining blood-alcohol content

- J -

- K -

- L -

lane change – lateral maneuver moving the vehicle from one lane to another using proper space management procedures

lane signal – a signal, usually overhead, indicating if a lane can or cannot be used at a specific time

liability insurance – provides compensation for damages which the insured is legally obligated to pay; covers others when you are at fault

light truck – a truck with a manufacturer's rated carrying capacity of not more than 2,000 lbs., including a pick up truck, panel delivery truck, and carry-all truck

limited use lanes – traffic flow lanes posted and designed to accommodate special vehicles or carpools

- M -

median – area of ground separating traffic moving in opposite directions

merging area – stretch of road at the end of an acceleration lane on an expressway where vehicles join the flow of traffic

minimum speed limit – speed limit to keep traffic moving safely by not allowing drivers to drive slower than a certain speed

moped – a motor-driven cycle that cannot attain a speed in one mile of more than 30 mph and the engine:
1. Cannot produce more than two-brake horsepower; and
2. If an internal combustion engine, has a piston displacement of 50 cubic centimeters or less and connects to a power drive system that does not require the operator to shift gears. Two-wheeled vehicle that can be driven with either a motor or pedal.

motorcycle – a motor vehicle, other than a tractor, equipped with a rider's saddle and designed to have when propelled not more than three wheels on the ground

- N -

night blindness – not being able to see well at night

no-fault insurance – covers an insured's losses and expenses associated with a collision regardless of fault

- O -

odometer – the device on the instrument panel indicating the total number of miles the vehicle has been driven

over driving headlights – driving at a speed making your stopping distance longer than the distance lighted by your headlights; low beams are limited to 45 mph and high beams are limited to 65 mph for stopping purposes

oversteer – when the rear tire patches lose varying degrees of traction and the front tire patches have more traction causing a spinning effect (yaw) around the vehicle's center of gravity. The vehicle has a tendency to spin to the left or right even though the driver is not turning the steering wheel

overtake – to pass the vehicle ahead

over-the-counter medicine – drug that can be obtained legally without a doctor's prescription

- P -

parallel parking – the vehicle lines up parallel or going the same direction as the curb. When parallel parking, the vehicle must be 6 to 18 inches from the curb

passive restraint device – a restraint device, such as an airbag or an automatic safety belt, that works without the passenger or driver initiating the device

pedestrian – a person on foot

pedestrian signal – a signal used at traffic intersections that indicates when a person should walk or wait

peer pressure – mental and social influence of others of a similar age on decision-making skills

perception distance – the distance your vehicle travels during perception time

perception time – the length of time it takes for the driver to make a risk-reduction decision

peripheral vision – the area a person can see that is around the central field of vision

perpendicular parking – the vehicle is parked at a right angle to a curb or parking stripe using visual reference points for entering and leaving

prescription medicine – drug that can be purchased legally only when ordered by a doctor

preventive maintenance – routine care and attention to your vehicle

property-damage insurance – protects the driver who is at fault against claims for damages to another person's property, up to specified limits

protected left turn – left turn made on a left-turn, green arrow, or delayed green light while oncoming traffic is stopped

protective gear – the items a motorcyclist wears to protect head, eyes, and body

- Q -

- R -

race – the use of one or more vehicles in an attempt to:

1. Out gain or outdistance another vehicle or prevent another vehicle from passing;
2. Arrive at a given destination ahead of another vehicle(s); or
3. Test the physical stamina or endurance of an operator over a long-distance driving route

reaction distance – the distance a vehicle travels from the point the driver perceives the need to act and the point where the driver takes action through braking, steering, or acceleration. Distance your vehicle travels until the driver perceives the need to change speed or position

reaction time – the time the vehicle travels from the point the driver perceives the need to act and the point where the driver takes the action through braking, steering, or acceleration. Length of time it takes the driver to execute a reduced-risk action, after a response is perceived by the driver

reduced visibility – the inability of a driver to see clearly

reference point – a part of the outside or inside of a vehicle, as viewed from the driver's seat, that relates to some part of the road which allows the driver to estimate position on the road. The road positions (points of reference) of the vehicle assist the driver in determining when to start turning, vehicle limitations, or where the vehicle is actually located

regulatory sign – a sign controlling traffic

restraint device – any part of a vehicle holding an occupant in the seat during a collision

restricted interlock license – authorizes an individual to operate a motor vehicle equipped with an ignition interlock device

revocation – the termination of a driver license or privilege for an indefinite period of time. May be restored when all requirements for the revocation have been satisfied

right of way – privilege of having immediate use of a certain part of a road

right turn on red – turning right when the red signal is on, after stopping behind the intersection guides, unless specifically prohibited to turn

roadway marking – markings and lane delineators (reflectors) providing you with warning or direction

rocking a vehicle – repeating the sequence of driving forward a little then back a little to move your vehicle out of deep snow, mud, or sand

rumble strips – sections of rough pavement intended to alert drivers of approaching roadway construction, tollbooth plaza, or other traffic conditions

- S -

safety belt – a lap belt and any shoulder straps included as original equipment on or added to a vehicle

safety chains – backup link used in case a trailer hitch fails

school zone – portion of a street or highway near a school subject to special speed limits

shared left-turn lane – the lane on a busy street helping drivers make safe mid-block left turns into business areas from a center lane

skid – occurs when tire patches lose part or all of their traction on the roadway surface due to abrupt suspension balance or roadway surfaces conditions

skid mark – a mark on the road surface from a tire sliding due to a loss of traction from braking or abrupt steering

slow-moving vehicle – the vehicle is unable to travel at highway speed

speed smear – occurs when objects in your peripheral vision become blurred and distorted as your speed increases

staggered stop – stopping when the white line visually disappears under the hood line. This allows extra space for left-turning vehicles

standard reference point – point which allows for vehicle placement on a road typical for most drivers

stimulant – drug that speeds up the central nervous system

stopping position – stopping behind a vehicle in a position allowing the driver enough space to steer around the vehicle to avoid a stalled, turning, or backing vehicle

suspension – the temporary withdrawal of a driver license or privilege for a definite period of time

- T -

tailgate – to follow another vehicle too closely

total stopping distance – the distance your vehicle travels while you make a stop

traction – friction or gripping power between the tire patches and the road surface

traffic circle – the intersections that form when several roads meet at a circle

traffic control devices – any signal, sign, or pavement marking used to control the movement of traffic

traffic signal – any signal used to control the movement of traffic

tunnel vision – the ability to see in a narrow field of vision of 140 degrees or less with little effective peripheral vision

turn – vehicle maneuver to change direction to the left or right

turnabout – the maneuvers for turning into or out of a road/driveway using reference points for positioning

- U -

uncontrolled intersection – an intersection that has no signs or signals to regulate traffic including railroad crossings that do not have flashing red lights or crossing gates

under-insured motorist insurance – covers costs exceeding the amount the other person's insurance company will pay as a result of a collision caused by another's fault

uninsured motorist insurance – covers costs up to a certain amount if you are struck by another vehicle whose driver has no insurance

unprotected left turn – left turn made at a signal-controlled intersection without a special left turn light

urban district – the territory adjacent to and including a highway, if the territory is improved with structures used for business, industry, or dwelling houses and are located at intervals of less than 100 feet for a distance of at least one-quarter mile on either side of the highway

- V -

vehicle – a device, in, upon, or by which any person or property is or may be transported or drawn upon a highway, excepting devices used exclusively upon stationary rails or tracks

vehicle malfunctions – failures of the vehicle to perform as designed, such as tire, steering, suspension, acceleration, fuel, etc.

vehicle maintenance – the scheduled or unscheduled upkeep or repair of a vehicle

vehicle maneuvers – moving forward, moving backward, turning, lateral maneuvers, and turnabouts

visibility – the ability to see

- W -

warning sign – a sign alerting you to possible hazards and road conditions

warning light – an instrument panel light warning of a system malfunction and usually stays on while the system is malfunctioning

- X -

- Y -

yield – to allow another vehicle or roadway user to proceed first

- Z -

zero tolerance law – it is illegal for individuals who are under 21 years of age to drive with any measurable amount of alcohol in their blood

Appendix B: Driver License Offices

DPS offers appointments for in-person DL/ID services at more than 220 driver license offices (DLO) statewide. We have offices ranging from one person, part-time offices to mega centers that offer up to 25 service counters, provide more flexible hours and employ more License and Permit Specialists to serve customers.

We encourage customers to utilize alternative service options such as online, telephone, or mail-in renewals when eligible. The department is working to make more service options available online to reduce the number of required DLO visits. We are also expanding third party education and testing options to provide more flexibility to customers who are getting a license for the first time.

All in person DL/ID services are provided by scheduled appointment.

Visit the DPS website at https://www.dps.texas.gov/DriverLicense/appointments.htm to find an office near you and schedule your appointment. Appointments may be booked up to six months in advance. Select the option to schedule a driver license appointment and follow the instructions to make your appointment. If you are unable to keep your appointment, please cancel it so other customers may be served promptly.

Visit the DPS website at https://www.dps.texas.gov/DriverLicense/ for the latest information about driver license offices and services.

Appendix C

Study and Review Questions for Class C Operators

1. What is the minimum age at which you can get a Class C driver license without either driver education or being a hardship case? *(Chpt. 1)*

2. How much is the maximum fine for a first conviction of driving without a license? *(Chpt. 1)*

3. What type of restrictions may be placed on your license? *(Chpt. 1)*

4. In what direction should you turn your wheels when parking uphill without a curb? *(Chpt. 7)*

5. What action should you take if you fail to receive the renewal notice card reminding you that your driver license is about to expire? *(Chpt. 1)*

6. On a one-way street, what color is the broken lane marker? *(Chpt. 5)*

7. Describe the "Yield" sign. *(Chpt. 5)*

8. What does a "Narrow Bridge" sign look like, and how should the driver react when he sees one? *(Chpt. 5)*

9. What is the shape of a "Keep Right" sign, and how should the driver react when he sees one? *(Chpt. 5)*

10. Which sign tells you to slow down because you are approaching a double curve? *(Chpt. 5)*

11. What does a "Do Not Pass" sign mean? *(Chpt. 5)*

12. Which sign tells you to keep in the right-hand lane when driving slow? *(Chpt. 5)*

13. What does "Yield Right-of-Way" mean? *(Chpt. 4, 5)*

14. Describe the equipment required on passenger cars by state law. *(Chpt. 2)*

15. What is the purpose of an exhaust emission system? *(Chpt. 2)*

16. Describe the types of equipment that Texas state law specifically forbids on passenger cars driven within the state. *(Chpt. 2)*

17. How should you react when a traffic officer tells you to do something that is ordinarily considered to be against the law? *(Chpt. 5)*

18. Once the brakes have been applied, about how many feet does a car which was going 70 mph travel before it comes to a stop? *(Chpt. 8)*

19. When is it necessary to stop before proceeding when you overtake a school bus loading or unloading children? *(Chpt. 4)*

20. About how many feet will the average driver going 50 mph travel from the moment he sees danger until he hits the brakes? *(Chpt. 8)*

21. Within how many feet of a crosswalk may you park, when parking near a corner? *(Chpt. 7)*

22. What is the state speed limit for automobiles in urban districts? *(Chpt. 8)*

23. Does a posted speed limit of 55 mph mean that you may drive 55 mph on that highway under all conditions? *(Chpt. 8)*

24. You should never drive on the left half of the roadway when you are within how many feet from an intersection, bridge, or railroad crossing? *(Chpt. 6)*

25. What should you do if you discover you are in the wrong lane to make a turn as you enter an intersection? *(Chpt. 6)*

26. When two cars meet at the intersection of a two-lane road with a four-lane road, which one must yield the right-of-way? *(Chpt. 4)*

27. If you are driving and hear a siren coming, what should you do? *(Chpt. 4)*

28. What is the first thing that should be done when a car starts to skid? *(Chpt. 9)*

29. At what time of the day should your headlights be turned on? *(Chpt. 9)*

30. Under what conditions may your driver license be suspended? *(Chpt. 1)*

31. What is carbon monoxide, and how may it be harmful to drivers? *(Chpt. 14)*

32. Describe what you should do if you have a blowout while driving. *(Chpt. 9)*

33. What should you do when driving down a steep grade in a car with standard transmission? *(Chpt. 9)*

34. What should you do if you damage an unattended vehicle? *(Chpt. 11)*

35. When are crash reports required? *(Chpt. 11)*

36. If you are required to show proof of financial responsibility for the future, how many years must such proof be kept up? *(Chpt. 3)*

37. What type of sign warns you to watch right and left for cross traffic? *(Chpt. 5)*

38. Describe the emblem that identifies vehicles which travel at speeds of 25 mph or less. *(Chpt. 5)*

39. In which gear should you drive when going down a steep hill? *(Chpt. 9)*

40. What qualifications must one have to teach a beginner to drive? *(Chpt. 1)*

41. If the person is under 18, when does his provisional license expire? *(Chpt. 1)*

42. When parked parallel, your curb side wheels must be no more than how many inches from the curb? *(Chpt. 7)*

43. When following another car, what is a good distance at which you should follow behind? *(Chpt. 8)*

44. To what agency and within what time period must a change of address be reported for driver licensing purposes? *(Chpt. 1)*

45. What effects does the use of marijuana and amphetamine have on driving? *(Chpt. 10)*

46. What is the penalty for being convicted of driving while intoxicated? *(Chpt. 10)*

47. What does a green arrow showing with a red light mean? *(Chpt. 5)*

48. How should you react to a flashing red light? *(Chpt. 5)*

49. Which sign tells you to watch out for a train? *(Chpt. 5)*

50. Describe the sign that warns you to slow down for a winding road. *(Chpt. 5)*

51. What sign indicates that the road that you are on merges with another? *(Chpt. 5)*

52. What kind of sign warns you that the highest safe speed for the turn ahead is 25 mph? *(Chpt. 5)*

53. Describe the sign that tells you to watch for cross traffic ahead. *(Chpt. 5)*

54. What type of sign warns you that you should slow down for a sharp rise in the roadway? *(Chpt. 5)*

55. Describe the type of sign that would let you know that you were on a short state highway in a city or urban area. *(Chpt. 5)*

56. What is the maximum number of inches you may lawfully allow an object to extend beyond the left fender of your car? *(Chpt. 2)*

57. Under what conditions must you always stop? *(Chpt. 5)*

58. What should you do when coming onto a street from a private alley or driveway? *(Chpt. 4)*

59. If a child runs into the road 45 to 50 feet ahead of your car, what is the highest speed from which you can stop with good brakes without hitting him? *(Chpt. 8)*

60. How close to a fireplug may a vehicle lawfully park? *(Chpt. 7)*

61. What does a posted speed limit of 55 mph mean? *(Chpt. 5)*

62. What is the maximum speed limit for passenger cars on a Texas Highway numbered by this state or United States outside an urban district? *(Chpt. 8)*

63. Under what circumstances should you never attempt to pass a car ahead of you? *(Chpt. 6)*

64. Under what conditions are overtaking and passing to the right not permitted? *(Chpt. 6)*

65. When a driver is waiting to make a left turn, what is the procedure he should take when the light turns green? *(Chpt. 5)*

66. What precautions should a driver take at uncontrolled intersections? *(Chpt. 4)*

67. What regulations should a bicycle rider observe? *(Chpt. 13)*

68. Under what conditions should headlights be used? *(Chpt. 9)*

69. You should dim your lights when you are within how many feet of an approaching car? *(Chpt. 9)*

70. What type of lighting should cars use when parked on the highway at night? *(Chpt. 9)*

71. Which lights should you use when you are driving in a fog? *(Chpt. 9)*

72. When are you required to show proof of financial responsibility? *(Chpt. 3)*

73. When needed, how may one show proof of financial responsibility? *(Chpt. 3)*

74. What sign warns you that you must slow down? *(Chpt. 5)*

75. What circumstances may lead to possible loss of your license? *(Chpt. 1)*

76. In addition to mufflers, what new equipment is required on all cars manufactured in 1968 and after? *(Chpt. 2)*

77. Why are seat belts important? *(Chpt. 14)*

78. What is meant by "defensive driving?" *(Chpt. 14)*

79. What are the different classes of licenses and age requirements for each? *(Chpt. 1)*

80. When is a bicyclist not required to ride to the right of the roadway? *(Chpt. 13)*

81. When are bicyclists allowed to ride two abreast in a traffic lane? *(Chpt. 13)*

82. What are the three most common motorist caused car-bicycle crashes? *(Chpt. 9)*

83. What are the penalties for minors (persons under the age of 21) convicted of Driving Under the Influence of Alcohol? *(Chpt. 10)*

84. What are the penalties for minors (persons under the age of 21) convicted of non-driving alcohol-related offenses? *(Chpt. 10)*

Appendix D: Fees

*A $1 administrative fee is included in the following fee amounts. If you are completing more than one transaction at the same time in person or online, you will only be charged this fee once. The $1 administrative fee is not charged for transactions conducted through the mail.

Driver License Fees

License type	*Fee	Information
Driver license (Class A, B or C)		
Under 18: new	$16	Expires on your 18th birthday
Age 18 to 84: new	$33	Expires after eight years (on your birthday)
Age 18 to 84: renewal	$33	Expires eight years after previous expiration date
Age 85 and older: new	$9	Expires after two years (on your birthday)
Age 85 and older: renewal	$9	Expires two years after previous expiration date
Disabled veterans (60%): new or renewal	Free	Requirements for fee exemption
Replacement driver license		
Replace a lost, stolen, or damaged license	$11	Current expiration date does not change
Change address or name		
Test to add or remove restrictions		
Learner license—under 18		
New	$16	Expires on your 18th birthday
Motorcycle with driver license (Class AM, BM or CM)		
Original Texas driver license with motorcycle	$48	Expires when your driver license expires (depends on age; see driver license section)
Renew driver license with motorcycle	$44	Expires when your driver license expires (depends on age; see driver license section)
Add motorcycle to existing driver license	$16	Expiration date on driver license does not change
Motorcycle license (Class M) only		
New	$33	Expiration date depends on age; see driver license section
Renewal	$44	Expiration date depends on age; see driver license section
Learner license for motorcycle (Class M) only		
Under 18	$16	Expires on your 18th birthday
Limited term driver license		
For temporary visitors to the US	$25	Expires when period of lawful presence expires, or in one year if lawful presence period is "duration of status"

Driver License Fees

License type	*Fee	Information
Occupational driver license		
New or renewal	$10 per year	Issued up to two years Must pay reinstatement fees first
Add interlock restriction to driver license	$10	Must pay reinstatement fees first
Driver license for individuals registered under Chapter 62, CCP		
New or renewal	$21	Expires one year after previous expiration date

Identification Card (ID) Fees

ID type	*Fee	Information
Identification (ID) card		
Age 59 and younger: new	$16	Expires after six years (on your birthday)
Age 59 and younger: renewal	$16	Expires six years after previous expiration date
Age 60 and older: new or renewal	$6	Expires six years after previous expiration date
Replacement ID card		
Replace a lost, stolen, or damaged ID card Change address or name	$11	Current expiration date does not change
Limited term ID card		
For temporary visitors to the U.S.	$16	Expires when period of lawful presence expires, or in one year if lawful presence period is "duration of status"
ID card for individuals registered under Chapter 62, CCP		
New or renewal	$21	Expires one year after previous expiration date

Appendix E: Restriction Codes

Code	Description
A	With corrective lenses
B	A licensed driver 21 years of age or older (LOFS) must be in the front seat
C	Daytime driving only
D	Speed not to exceed 45 mph
E	No manual transmission equipped CMV
F	Must hold valid learner license to MM/DD/YY
G	TRC 545.424 applies until MM/DD/YY
H	Vehicle not to exceed 26,000 lbs. GVWR
I	Motorcycle not to exceed 250cc
J	Licensed motorcycle operator 21 or over in sight
K	Intrastate only
L	No air brake equipped CMV
M	No Class A passenger vehicle
N	No Class A and B passenger vehicle
O	No tractor-trailer CMV
P	Stated on license
Q	A licensed driver 21 years of age or older (LOFS) must be in the front seat (vehicle above a Class B)
R	A licensed driver 21 years of age or older (LOFS) must be in the front seat (vehicle above a Class C)
S	Outside rearview mirror or hearing aid
T	Automatic transmission
U	Applicable prosthetic devices
V	Medical variance documents required
W	Power steering
X	No cargo in CMV tank vehicle
Y	Valid Texas vision or limb waiver required
Z	No full air brake equipped CMV
P1	For Class M TRC 545.424 until MM/DD/YY
P2	To/from work/school
P3	To/from work
P4	To/from school
P5	To/from work/school or a licensed driver 21 years of age or older (LOFS) must be in the front seat
P6	To/from work or a licensed driver 21 years of age or older (LOFS) must be in the front seat
P7	To/from school or a licensed driver 21 years of age or older (LOFS) must be in the front seat
P8	With telescopic lens
P9	A licensed driver 21 years of age or older (LOFS 21), bus only
P10	A licensed driver 21 years of age or older (LOFS 21), school bus only

Code	Description
P11	Bus not to exceed 26,000 GVWR
P12	Passenger CMVs restricted to Class C only
P13	A license driver 21 years of age or older (LOFS) in vehicle equip with air brake
P14	Operation Class B exempt vehicle authorized
P15	Operation Class A exempt vehicle authorized
P16	If CMV, school buses (interstate)
P17	If CMV, government vehicles (interstate)
P18	If CMV, only transporting personal property (interstate)
P19	If CMV, transporting corpse/sick/injured (interstate)
P20	If CMV, privately transporting passengers (interstate)
P21	If CMV, fire/rescue (interstate)
P22	If CMV, intra-city zone drivers (interstate)
P23	If CMV, custom harvesting (interstate)
P24	If CMV, transporting bees/hives (interstate)
P25	If CMV, use in oil/water well service/drill
P26	If CMV, for operation of mobile crane
P27	HME Expiration Date MM/DD/YY
P28	FRSI CDL valid MM/DD/YY to MM/DD/YY
P29	FRSI CDL MM/DD/YY–MM/DD/YY or exempt B vehicles
P30	FRSI CDL MM/DD/YY–MM/DD/YY or exempt A vehicles
P31	Class C only; no taxi/bus/emergency vehicle
P32	Other
P33	No passengers in CMV bus
P34	No express or highway driving
P35	Restricted to operation of three–wheeled MC
P36	Moped
P37	Occ/Essent need DL-no CMV–see court order
P38	Applicable vehicle devices
P39	Ignition Interlock required
P40	Vehicle not to exceed Class C

Made in the USA
Coppell, TX
04 April 2025

47899202R00050